CARDIOLOGY

Cavendish
Publishing
Limited

TITLES IN THE SERIES

CARDIOLOGY

Dr Roger Blackwood, MA, BM, BCh, FRCP

Consultant Cardiologist, Wexham Park &
Heatherwood Hospitals

Hon Consultant, Hammersmith Hospital

SERIES EDITOR

**Dr Walter Scott, LLB (Hons),
MBBS, MRCGP, DObstRCOG**

Cavendish
Publishing
Limited

First published in Great Britain 1996 by Cavendish Publishing Limited, The Glass House, Wharton Street, London WC1X 9PX.

Telephone: 0171-278 8000 Facsimile: 0171-278 8080

Blackwood, R
Cardiology for lawyers - (Medico-legal practitioner series)
1. Heart – Diseases – Law and legislation – England
I. Title
616.1'2'0024344

1-85941-213-0

Printed and bound in Great Britain

FOREWORD

Those who have shown an interest in the 'medico-legal practitioner's series' may like to learn something about its origins and the history of its development. With this objective in mind I will devote a few moments to the past and I will then turn to the future which is, after all, even more important for us.

I first conceived the idea of such a theme in the Summer of 1994. By that stage I had been preparing reports for lawyers on cases of alleged medical negligence for about five years. I had also been looking at other doctors' reports for the same length of time and it was becoming increasingly apparent to me that one of the lawyers' most difficult tasks was to understand the medical principles clearly. To be fair to the lawyers, there were some doctors who did not always make matters very clear. This, coupled with the difficulty which many doctors have in understanding the legal concept of negligence and related topics, merely served to compound the problem.

It therefore occurred to me that a possible solution to the difficulty would be to develop some material on medical topics written by doctors who had a particular interest in the medico-legal field. The authors would require at least four attributes. First, they would have to be specialists in their own field. Secondly, they would need the ability to explain their subject to non-medical readers in clear language that was easy to follow. Put another way there was no case for writing a medical textbook for their students or colleagues. Thirdly, they would require a fair amount of experience in medico-legal reporting, analysis of cases and dealing with lawyers who were defending or advancing cases. This would give them an understanding of how the lawyer's mind works and an appreciation of the medical areas which can cause difficulty in practice and where accidents can happen. There would be a contrast with medical books where the emphasis is on the diseases which most commonly present to the doctor. Fourthly, the authors would need the ability to work in harmony with a series editor who was anxious to achieve some degree of uniformity across the whole range of the material.

Having identified these four points as being desirable characteristics of the potential authors the next step was to find a publisher who would be sufficiently interested to give the project the support it needed. This was to be no small task and was likely to involve a very long term commitment because, after the initial launch, it was inevitable that much more work would be required by way of future editions and additional titles. I was most fortunate to be dealing with Cavendish Publishing in connection with my own book, *The General Practitioner and the Law of Negligence*, and I am pleased to say that they seized this new idea with the utmost enthusiasm. At last I thought that the 'medico-legal practitioner series' would become a reality.

It then only remained to find the authors, commission the work and wait for the results. It was at this point, however, that I began to realise that I was still only at the very beginning of my task. Eventually, however, after numerous discussions with various people a team materialised. When the early chapters of the first books began to arrive it was starting to look as though we really were going to have something which was quite unique. When the final manuscripts arrived my confidence increased still further. More than two years after my initial plans the first set of books has become available and the dream has turned into reality.

This, then, is how the project came into being but it must be emphasised that, in a manner of speaking, we have really only just got ourselves started. For the series to thrive it must be flexible and respond to the needs of its users. It must adapt to medical developments and legal changes. Clinical subjects are a primary consideration but it is my firm intention to expand the series to involve other areas of interest. Indeed the first non-clinical title should appear almost as soon as the initial set becomes available. On a more long term basis, I would like the series to cover every field of expertise that is of concern to the medico-legal practitioner.

Uniformity of approach and clarity of presentation must be hallmarks of the individual titles but the series as a whole must be independent and objective. If we can aspire to these criteria we should achieve a fair measure of success in assisting our readers to give good advice to their clients.

It remains for me to express my gratitude to all the authors and to the publishers for their cooperation. In another kind of way I will be equally grateful to all our readers for placing their reliance on us and for sharing our optimism.

Walter Scott
Series Editor
Slough
August 1996

PREFACE

The practice of medicine is more about anxiety than disease. Whether a patient has a cold or cancer it is the worry about what may happen that is as concerning as much as the underlying condition. Addressing this problem takes time – now very much at a premium for any doctor. Reducing waiting lists and waiting time is more important than being able to sit down and talk to the patient. The public is increasingly dissatisfied because its expectations have been magnified by the 'Patients Charter'. If patients do not get what they want litigation is in everybody's thoughts, especially since legal aid is known to be available. Nowadays, some person or being is responsible for any mishap – 'Acts of God' can no longer occur – and the doctor is increasingly on trial.

Roger Blackwood
September 1996

CONTENTS

Contents

CHAPTER ONE

ANATOMY AND PHYSIOLOGY

INTRODUCTION

The concept of the circulation of blood around the body was first described by W Harvey in *De Motu Cordis* in 1628. Because of it he was regarded as a virtual heretic and lost much of his private practice. Prior to Harvey it was thought that blood ebbed and flowed from the heart conveying vital and natural spirits. All this dated back to Galen in the second century who formed this view predominantly from animal dissection. Post-mortems on humans were forbidden by Roman regulations at this time.

That such an erroneous view of the functions of the human body should exist for 1400 years indicates the conservative nature of medicine and the lack of scientific investigation through the Dark Ages. Serventus, who almost proposed the circulation of the blood in 1553, was burned at the stake (slowly) for his views. The advent of dissection of human bodies in medical schools throughout Europe from 1600 onwards, particularly by Versalius, confirmed Harvey's theory, and the beginnings of modern medicine had started.

CIRCULATION OF THE BLOOD

The circulation of blood around the body and through the lungs is shown in diagrammatic form in Figure 1. Blood returns from the body to the heart via

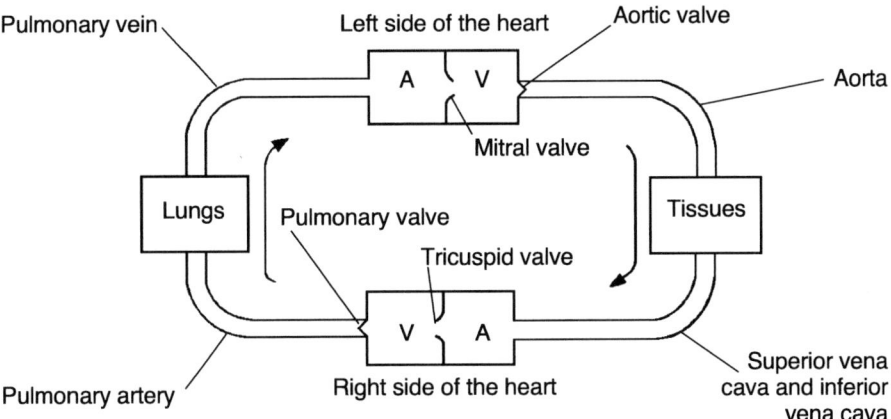

Figure 1. Schematic diagram of the circulation showing the four heart valves during ventricular diastole (A = atrium; V = ventricle).

the superior or inferior vena cava into the right atrium, and passes through the tricuspid valve in to the right ventricle. The right ventricle pumps blood into the lungs via the pulmonary artery. Having picked up oxygen, blood returns via the pulmonary veins to the left atrium and through the mitral valve to the left ventricle. This is the main pumping chamber of the body which pumps blood from the left ventricle, at considerable pressure, through the aortic valve into the aorta and via various blood vessels to the tissues. It should be noted that, if the atria fail to contract, circulation can still occur and is very little impaired. If the ventricles cease to work, circulation of blood ceases immediately.

THE HEART

Figure 2 shows the heart with its normal anatomy. The position of the heart is predominantly behind the sternum. The apex of the heart lies in the fifth left intercostal space and in the mid-clavicular line. The superior aspect of the heart where the vessels enter is called the base and the extremity of the ventricles is termed the apex. The pressure in the left atrium is generally very low – between 0–6mmHg. The pressure in the pulmonary artery is approximately 30/15mmHg, which is sufficient to pump the blood through the lungs and thence to the pulmonary veins.

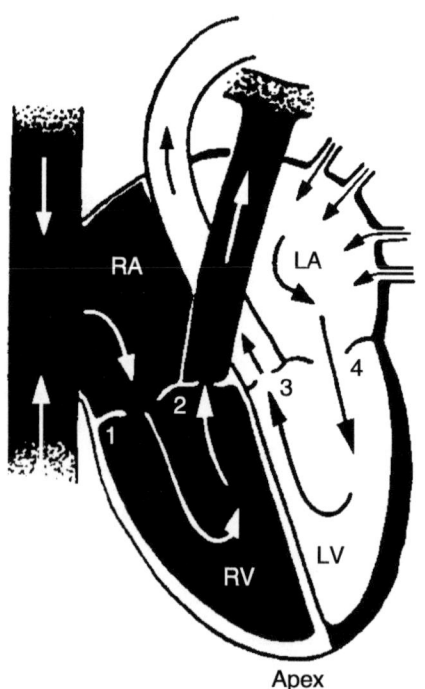

1.	Tricuspid valve
2.	Pulmonary valve
3	Aortic valve
4.	Mitral valve
RA	Right atrium
LA	Left atrium
RV	Right ventricle
LV	Left ventricle

Figure 2. The normal anatomy of the heart.

When blood reaches the left atrium its pressure is a mean of approximately 12mmHg. In the left ventricle the peak pressure in the normal man is about 120mmHg and at the end of the ejection phase drops to below 20mmHg. Once the blood has reached the aorta, the peak pressure remains the same as the left ventricle, ie about 120mmHg. However, because of the elastic recoil of the aorta and other major blood vessels, the diastolic pressure is maintained higher and is normally about 80mmHg.

The ejection phase of blood from the heart is known as systole and the relaxation phase when the ventricles fill with blood is known as diastole. The amount of blood ejected with each beat is known as the stroke volume (about 70cc), and the quantity circulated each minute is called the cardiac output (about 5 litres/min at rest, rising to 30 litres/min at maximum exercise).

ELECTRICAL ACTIVITY OF THE HEART

A wave of electricity flows through the heart muscle, followed by contraction. The electrical activity originates in the sino-atrial (SA) node and flows like a wave over both atria. From this point electricity can only enter the ventricles in a normal patient via the atrio-ventricular node. From the AV node an

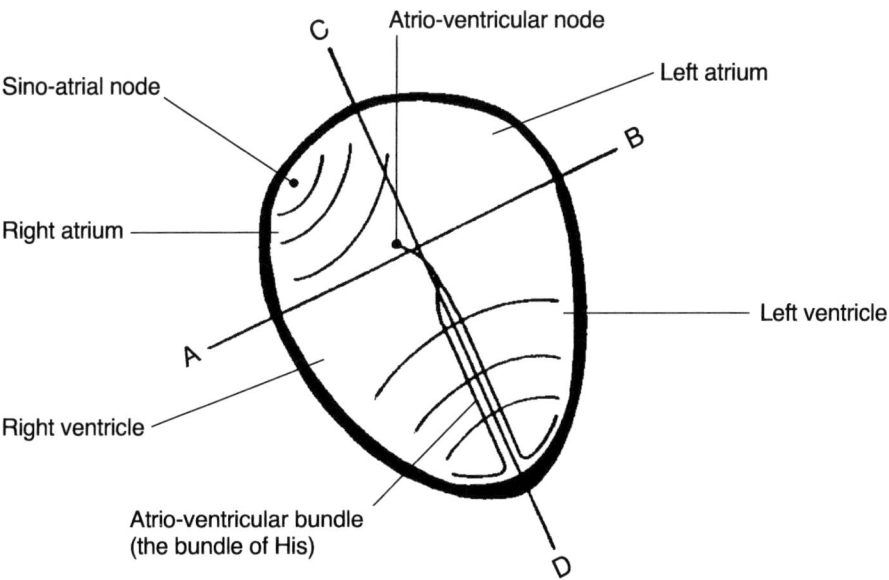

Figure 3. The spread of the cardiac impulse from the pacemaker (sinu-atrial node) through the atrial muscle to the atrio-ventricular node. It reaches the ventricular muscle via the atrio-ventricular bundle. A–B is the plane of the fibrous septum between the atria and the ventricles. C–D is the plane between the right and left chambers of the heart.

electrical wiring system is present, allowing depolarisation to be rapidly conducted to the apex of the ventricles so that contraction begins from the lower part of the ventricles rather than the upper part. If the upper part of the heart contracted first, blood would become trapped in the ventricle. The wave of electricity flowing over the heart is known as depolarisation and the wave of electricity returning to the SA node is known as depolarisation.

THE PERICARDIUM

The heart lies in a sac known as the pericardium, which consists of fibrous material. It prevents over-distention of the heart and, because it is richly supplied with pain fibres, provides a protection for the heart.

HEART SOUNDS

There are two basic heart sounds and a considerable number of additional ones. The first is coincidental with the closure of the mitral and tricuspid valves, although not due directly to this. The second heart sound is coincidental with the pulmonary and aortic valves closing. The third heart sound is created by the rapid influx of blood from the atrium into the ventricle in the first part of diastole, and is common in normal people. The fourth heart sound is probably created by the sudden stretching of the left ventricle by atrial contraction at the end of diastole. This usually represents a degree of heart failure. Valve clicks can also occur from the rapid opening of both the pulmonary and aortic valves, and an opening snap can occur when a scarred mitral valve opens suddenly against pressure.

CORONARY ARTERIES

The heart's own blood supply comes from two major coronary arteries (Figure 4). The right coronary artery supplies the right atrium and right ventricle and, to a variable extent, the intraventricular septum and inferior surface of the left ventricle. The left coronary artery begins as the left main stem and divides into two major branches. The left anterior descending coronary artery runs down the anterior surface of the heart supplying the anterior part of the left ventricle. Much of the intraventricular septum and the circumflex artery runs to the back of the heart supplying structures there. The first inch of the left coronary artery, known as the left main stem, may become narrowed with atheroma, and this can be particularly dangerous. There are veins in the heart which run in parallel with the main arteries and then drain into the coronary sinus, and thus directly into the right atrium.

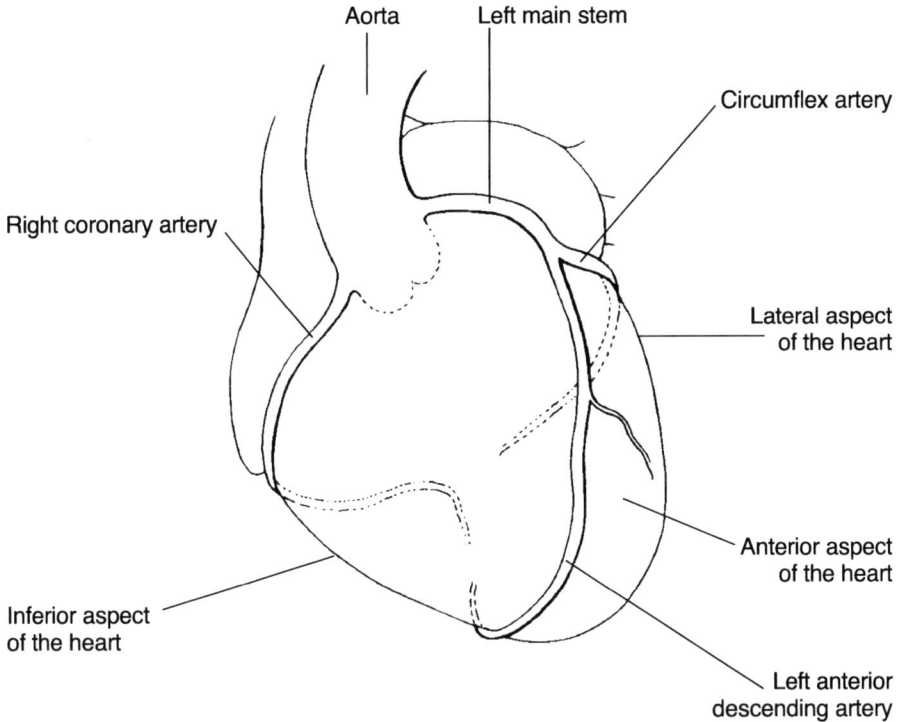

Figure 4. The coronary arteries.

PHYSIOLOGICAL CONTROL OF THE HEART

There are two basic control mechanisms of the heart, intrinsic (from within the heart) and extrinsic (from outside it).

(a) Intrinsic control – when the amount of blood returning to the heart increases it will stimulate the heart to work harder and increase cardiac output. This will also occur if the left atrial pressure rises. This particular type of pressure is known as pre-load. Increasing the pre-load increases cardiac output up to a certain maximum level. If the systemic blood pressure should rise, the cardiac output will decrease. This is known as the after-load. Both sides of the heart are controlled by the same mechanism, so that the same stroke volume occurs in the left and right ventricles simultaneously. Otherwise the lungs would rapidly fill with blood and the right ventricle would cease to function.

(b) Extrinsic control – there is, in effect, a brake and accelerator of the heart. The braking mechanism is the Vagus nerve, known as the para-sympathetic nervous supply. Stimulation of this slows the heart to varying degrees and, during a common faint, will slow it so much that the blood ceases to circulate. The accelerator system of the heart is related to adrenaline and similar substances known as cathelcholamines. Not only does this cause an increase in heart rate, it also increases the heart contractility so that there is a greater cardiac output. This side of the mechanism is known as the sympathetic nervous system. Heart rates, therefore, are controlled by a balance of the parasympathetic and sympathetic nervous systems.

BLOOD VESSELS

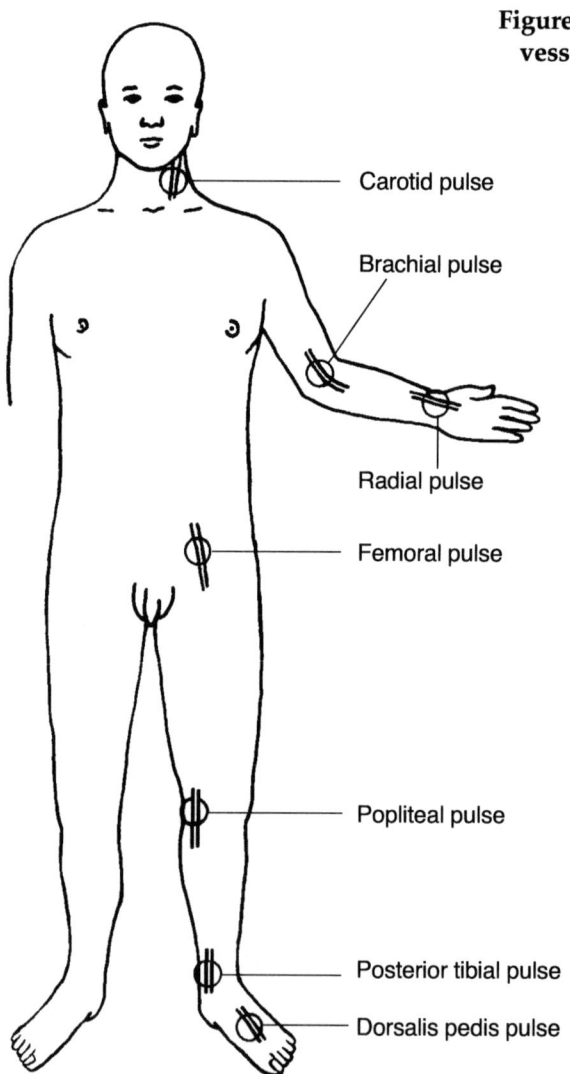

Figure 5. The main blood vessels easily palpated.

Carotid pulse

Brachial pulse

Radial pulse

Femoral pulse

Popliteal pulse

Posterior tibial pulse

Dorsalis pedis pulse

The aorta leading from the heart is approximately of 1in diameter. Main blood vessels such as the subclavian, carotid and femoral are of about 0.5in diameter, and subsequently the arteries get smaller, becoming arterioles and eventually capillaries. The main blood vessels which can be palpated are seen in Figure 5.

If turbulence occurs within an artery due, eg, to narrowing from atheroma, the sound which can be heard with a stethoscope is called a bruit. This may be heard in the neck when a patient has had a stroke.

A localised dilatation of the blood vessel is known as an aneurysm. The commonest site for this would be in the abdominal aorta, and once it reaches a certain size (>5.5cm) it may need to be operated upon or it may rupture. Because the arteries consist of three layers, a condition can occur called dissection. This is where blood tracks in between two of the layers of the arterial wall which can create great pain, but can also close off branch arteries so that blood ceases to flow to a particular organ, eg the kidney.

CHAPTER TWO

SYMPTOMS OF HEART DISEASE

INTRODUCTION

History is of the greatest importance in cardiology. The diagnosis of angina pectoris, for example, is made strictly on the history alone and not on examination. Cardiovascular disease may, however, be quite severe without any symptoms, and a patient who has severe anginal pain may feel completely well between the attacks. Patients with heart disease seldom actually feel 'ill'.

DYSPNOEA

Dyspnoea is shortness of breath. It is a very subjective symptom and varies enormously from one patient to another. The exact mechanism in heart disease is not known, but is probably related to the engorgement of the pulmonary vessels with blood making the lungs very stiff. Breathlessness is normally graded according to New York Heart Association Classification.

Grade 1	Asymptomatic
Grade 2	Symptoms obvious on moderate exercise
Grade 3	Symptoms obvious on mild exercise
Grade 4	Symptoms at rest

Dyspnoea is probably the commonest cardiac symptom, but in itself does not suggest a specific lesion. Dyspnoea may occur very late in a disease as in aortic stenosis, when its presence is prognostically serious, but usually its severity gradually increases with that of the lesion.

Sudden dyspnoea may suggest acute heart failure, an acute chest infection, pneumothorax or a pulmonary embolus. Variable breathlessness is usually psychogenic in origin and is often accompanied by an inability to get enough air in to the lungs and periodic deep sighing. Nervously induced, excessive breathlessness is known as hyperventilation.

ORTHOPNOEA

Orthopnoea is the sense of breathlessness when lying flat. When lying down there is as much as half a litre more blood in the lungs compared with standing. In a patient with heart disease the lungs become stiffer and this will produce breathlessness. The patient will tend to sleep on four or five pillows or sitting in a chair.

PAROXYSMAL NOCTURNAL DYSPNOEA

This is a situation where a patient awakes from sleep gasping for breath and with a feeling of suffocation. It is caused by the same mechanism as orthopnoea, but is much more acute and severe. Typically the patient sits up in bed and goes to the window to get cool air. It is a serious sign indicating significant heart failure.

CHEST PAIN

Figure 6 shows the various types of chest pain which exist. The exact history of the chest pain is clearly of considerable importance, but the overwhelming diagnosis which must be made is whether it is cardiac in origin or not.

Although cardiac pain will be dealt with in greater detail in later chapters, it consists of angina pectoris, unstable angina or a myocardial infarction. Angina pectoris is retrosternal tight chest pain associated with exercise or emotion, radiating sometimes to the left arm and occasionally to the neck and jaw and right arm. It is relieved by rest and is made worse in windy and cold weather, as well as after a heavy meal.

Figure 6 (below and right). Causes of chest pain.

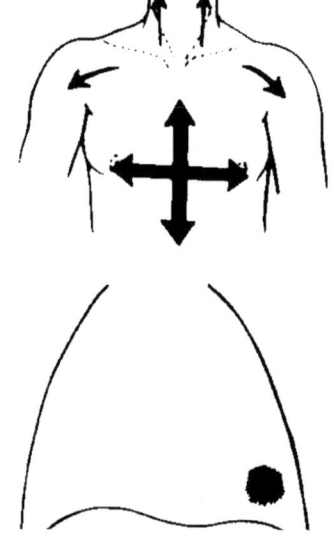

Myocardial
Constricting, severe retrosternal pain radiating to throat and arms. Sweating and dyspnoea. Usual cause is myocardial infarction, but consider dissecting aneurysm (if pain goes through to back).

Pericardial
Central, sharp on breathing, eased by certain positions, eg sitting forward.
? Pericardial rub.

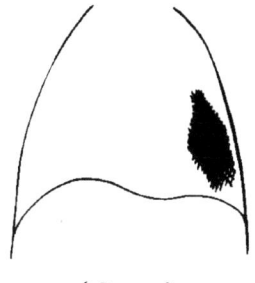

Pleuritic

Sharp, catches on breathing and coughing.
Dyspnoea.
? Pleural rub.

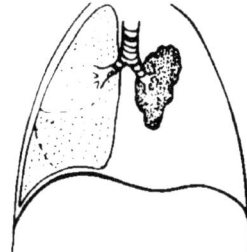

Pneumothorax

Sharp, catches on breathing and coughing.
Dyspnoeic. Cyanosis, collapse and severe
dyspnoea if tension pneumothorax.

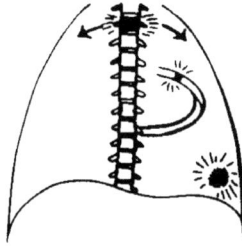

Musculo-skeletal

Localised pain.

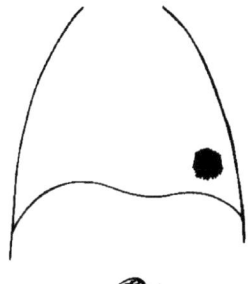

Cardiac neurosis

Left sided, stabbing, no relation to exercise.
Dyspnoea and palpitations common.
Depression.

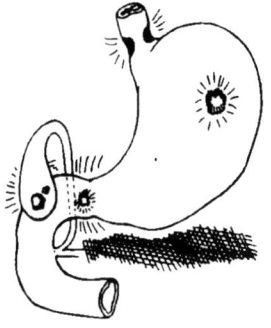

Gastrointestinal

Hiatus hernia, gastric ulcer, pacreatitis,
duodenal ulcer, gall bladder disease.

The chest pain of unstable angina is usually central, crushing, but continuous and often coming on at rest. It usually lasts for 5–20min, and may become increasingly severe over a matter of weeks or days.

The most severe form of cardiac pain is that of a heart attack or myocardial infarction where the pain generally lasts for more than half an hour. It is central and crushing, associated with sweat and pallor.

A tablet of glyceryl trinitrate under the tongue can be useful in diagnosis because it dilates blood vessels and relieves angina. However, it also relaxes other smooth muscles such as that of the oesophagus, and cannot be taken as an absolute sign of angina.

The patient who draws his hand across his chest in describing the pain may have angina, whereas one who points to it with one finger seldom does so.

Pericardial pain can be very similar to myocardial pain, but tends to be eased in certain positions, eg sitting forward. The chest pain of cardiac neurosis, also known as Da Costa's syndrome (after the doctor who described it in the American civil war), is usually left sided, stabbing and with no relation to exercise. Breathlessness and palpitations are common with it, and the patient looks depressed. This is not an infrequent pain in modern society.

PALPITATIONS

The word palpitations refers to an awareness of the heart beating. It does not imply any particular type of heart rhythm and can refer to sudden extra beats, episodes where the heart seems to miss a beat or episodes where the heart is racing, and so on. It is often difficult to diagnose the exact nature of palpitations without an ECG, but it is a common phenomenon and by no means always suggests heart disease.

LIGHTHEADEDNESS

Heart problems may cause light headedness, which must be distinguished from dizziness. Lightheadedness is a feeling that one might faint, whilst dizziness (also called vertigo) is an awareness of the world spinning around. Abnormal heart rhythms can cause lightheadedness, but it is brain problems that cause vertigo.

SYNCOPE

Syncope is the sudden cessation of consciousness which can be caused by many factors including both the heart and brain. The heart can cause syncope without warning as in the development of heart block, or gradually, eg when a fast rhythm becomes increasingly difficult for the heart to cope with. There is an enormous number of causes of syncope including cardiac arrhythmias, abnormal heart valves, heart failure, congenital heart disease and massive pulmonary embolus. Any form of syncope must be taken seriously, although the diagnosis of it is sometimes difficult, often requiring considerable perseverance.

Included in syncope is the common faint. This is where the heart slows suddenly, decreasing cardiac output, and is due to the stimulation of the braking mechanism of the heart (the vagus nerve). This can happen from pain, shock or fear. Curiously, people seem to faint more frequently in restaurants and churches. Due to the embarrassment of such a situation, the onlookers tend to try and sit the patient back up in the chair. This tends to worsen the situation by preventing any blood from reaching the brain. The correct procedure is to lie the patient down until recovery, which usually happens within half to one minute. When recovering, the patient will frequently feel awful and nauseated.

OEDEMA

Oedema is the collection of fluid outside tissue spaces, which can result from many causes but in particular can occur in heart failure. Oedema in the lungs causes breathlessness, especially when lying down. In chronic situations the influence of gravity causes fluid to descend towards the ankles and the feet, causing swelling. Diuretics or 'water tablets' make the kidneys pass excess water and help to get rid of oedema.

COUGH

Cough associated with heart disease is usually dry and non-productive. Occasionally, as in severe heart failure, the cough can be associated with sputum mixed with blood. Drugs such as ACE inhibitors can sometimes be associated with a dry cough. The coughing up of blood (haemoptysis) may occur with pulmonary embolism.

FATIGUE

Fatigue is common in any illness and in daily life. However, if a patient is clearly sleeping longer, or describes himself as exhausted compared with say one year previously, it must be taken seriously and might be related to heart disease.

CHAPTER THREE

CARDIAC INVESTIGATIONS

INTRODUCTION

While history-taking and examination is the start of all diagnoses, cardiac investigations are required in most cases in order to reach an exact diagnosis, formulate a correct treatment pattern and indicate a prognosis. The ECG and cardiac X-ray can be performed by the GP, but all other tests are normally carried out in hospital. Non-invasive tests, eg echocardiography and exercise tests, are generally carried out in district general hospitals, and invasive tests, eg cardiac catheterisation, are usually performed in teaching hospitals.

ECG

In the 1860s Lord Burdon Sanderson discovered that electricity flowed down the heart of a frog from top to bottom and was followed by contraction. In 1880, Waller from University College in London recorded the first ECG from man, and the whole format of presenting ECGs, which are identical to those used today, was produced by Sir Thomas Lewis, also from University College Hospital, between 1910 and 1920.

The ECG is a standard test throughout the world, recording a signal of approximately 1mV at a speed of either 25 or 50mm/sec. Ten electrode pads are attached to the patient in different positions, ie right arm, left arm, left leg, right leg and across the chest. From various combinations of the electrodes, 12 different lead recordings are made. Six leads (I, II, III, AVR, AVL and AVF) look at the heart in the vertical plane and six leads look in the horizontal plane (V1–6) (see Figure 7, page 16).

When the ECG is recorded, each complex is scrutinised, and the type of electrical rhythm is identified. The ECG in the normal person inevitably varies within certain normal limits, and it must be emphasised that these normal limits are very widespread, making the interpretation of the ECG difficult. The variety of electrical impulses that can be produced are indicated by the size of the standard text books on ECG complexes. The basic ECG complex is shown in Figure 8 (page 17).

The flow of electricity (depolarisation) starting at the sinus node and spreading over the atria produces the P-wave and then the QRS complex when it subsequently spreads over the ventricles. Electricity returning to the sinus node (repolarisation) produces the T-wave. Each of the 12 ECG leads will have a slightly different P-QRS-T complex.

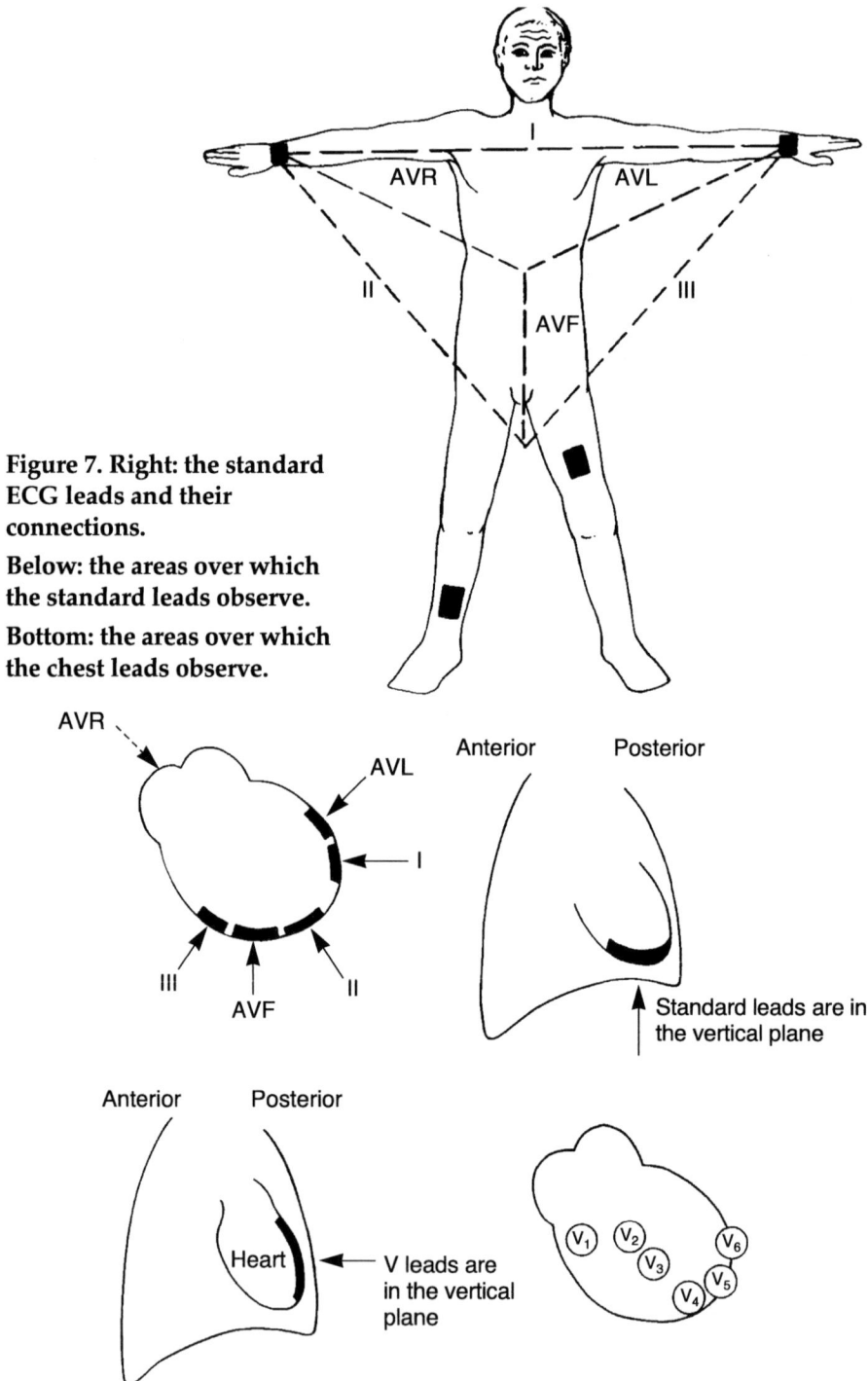

Figure 7. Right: the standard ECG leads and their connections.

Below: the areas over which the standard leads observe.

Bottom: the areas over which the chest leads observe.

Standard leads are in the vertical plane

V leads are in the vertical plane

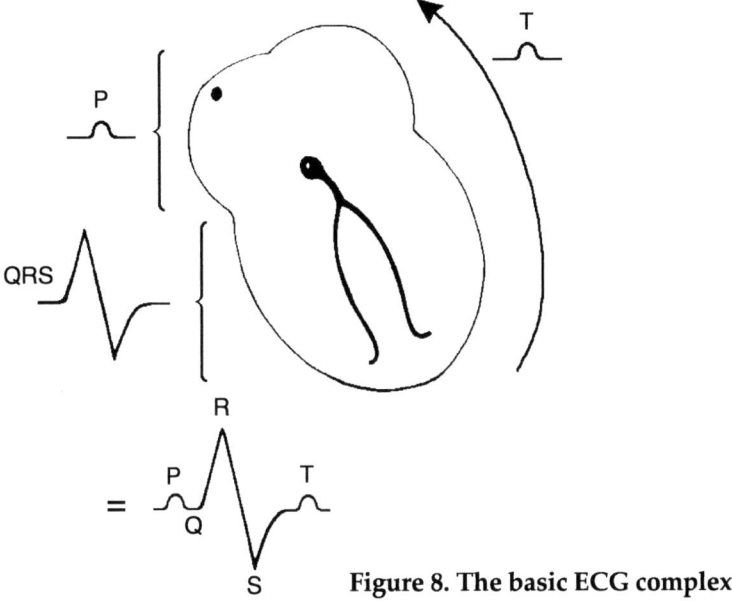

Figure 8. The basic ECG complex.

The ECG is performed with the patient lying comfortably and with standard leads attached to the legs or body and the V leads attached to the front of the chest. Most ECG machines record all 12 leads automatically. It is quite easy to produce a poor quality ECG tracing such as a distorted baseline, but most ECGs should be of a high quality. The ECG can record an enormous variety of different traces, some of which are as follows.

Evidence of ischaemic heart disease

This is probably its most important use. It can detect ischaemia (lack of oxygen to the tissue), an injury pattern of heart muscle or dead myocardium, all of which may occur during a heart attack. Ischaemia is usually shown by an alteration of the T-wave (inverted), injury by a raised ST segment and dead tissue by Q-waves. Quite severe ischaemic patterns can be shown by depressed ST segments, and there are many other subtle changes (Figure 9).

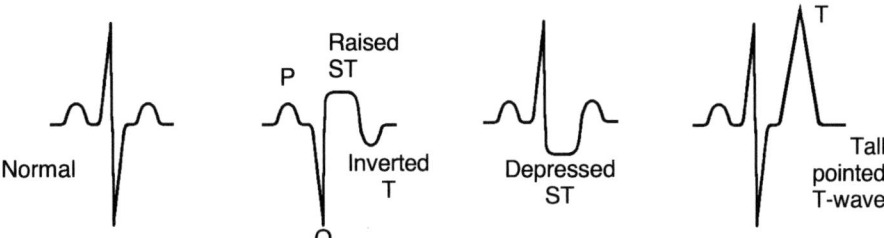

Figure 9. Ischaemia patterns.

Hypertrophy

Hypertrophy is an increase or thickening of the heart muscle and can develop in all chambers. The most important chamber which hypertrophies is the left ventricle, which can occur, for example, in high blood pressure, aortic stenosis and hypertrophic cardiomyopathy. The ECG is not the most sensitive test for hypertrophy, but is very useful.

Tachycardias (fast heart rates)

There is a considerable variety of fast heart rates which can be delineated by the ECG. Perhaps the most common is an irregular heart rate called atrial fibrillation, which affects 10% of the population after the age of 70. Some tachycardias are of little danger to the heart, eg atrial flutter, whereas others may be dangerous, eg ventricular tachycardia.

Bradycardias (slow heart rates)

A slow heart rate is not necessarily harmful and is often present in an athlete. Some Olympic athletes are known to walk around with pulses of only 28. A slow pulse is also typical during fainting. More serious, slower heart rates can be a symptom of heart block, which may require a pacemaker.

Ectopics

A beat originating from any other part of the heart except the sino-atrial node is known as an ectopic beat. These can come from the atrial area, around the A-V node or the ventricle. They are known respectively as atrial, junctional and ventricular ectopics. They are seldom serious, but frequently worrying to the patient (see Figure 10).

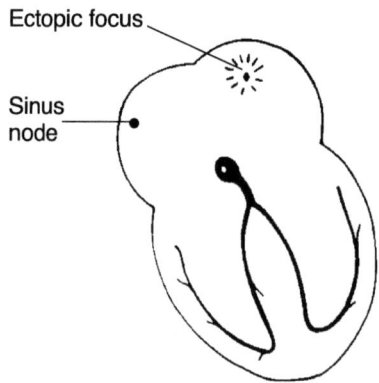

Ectopic focus

Sinus node

P P P

P

Atrial ectopic   Compensatory pause

Figure 10. Above: The ectopic focus.
Top of page 19: an ECG showing the ectopic beat

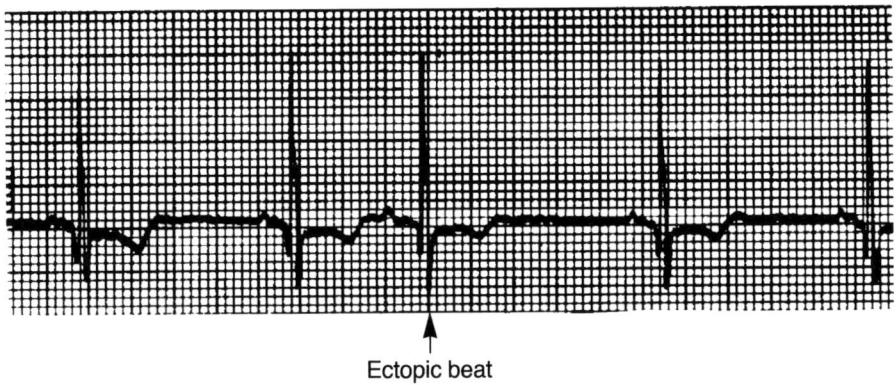

Ectopic beat

THE EXERCISE TEST

An ECG recorded during exercise is of most value in the diagnosis of ischaemic heart disease and the delineation of chest pain. A patient starts walking on a treadmill at approximately 1mph up a 1 in 10 slope and, after five three-minute intervals, reaches almost 5mph up a 1 in 5 slope. This is known as the Bruce protocol and is standard for exercise tests throughout the world. Occasionally a bicycle with gradation of exercise is used instead of a treadmill, to similar effect. In this country we largely use a treadmill, whilst on the continent the bicycle is more favoured.

The exercise test is generally very safe, but in the wrong situation is potentially dangerous and should only be performed by experienced personnel. An exercise test is deemed positive if the exercise is accompanied by chest pains, a significant drop in blood pressure, the occurrence of arrhythmias or electrical changes on ECG such as depressed ST segments (see Figure 11). This type of test is by no means infallible. The results of many tests may be hotly debated, but it is reasonable to say that the greater the ST segment depression, the greater the likelihood of ischaemic heart disease. An ST segment depression of 1mm may well not be ischaemic heart disease, whereas 4–5mm of ST segment depression might indicate quite dangerous ischaemia. In fit young men with no evidence of heart disease who take the exercise tests, up to 20% have false positive results.

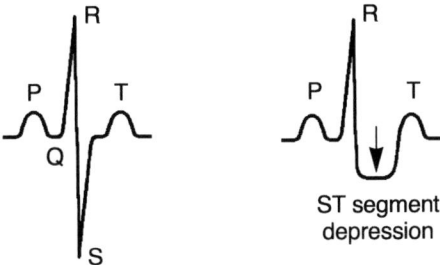

Figure 11. ST segment changes

24–48 HOUR ECG RECORDING

A patient with dizzy spells, funny turns, palpitations or blackouts may have a cardiac arrhythmia, but it is seldom possible to record this because there is usually so little warning of an event that it is over by the time a conventional ECG is performed. To record an arrhythmia, a patient can wear a small recorder attached to his waistband, recording the ECG either on a tape or digitally (Figure 12). The patient carries out his normal activities and wears it whilst asleep. If the symptoms occur during the time the patient is being monitored, a diagnosis can usually be made. After the patient has worn the machine for 24–48 hours, the tape or machine is linked to a computer which analyses the data and prints out information on any adverse events which occurred.

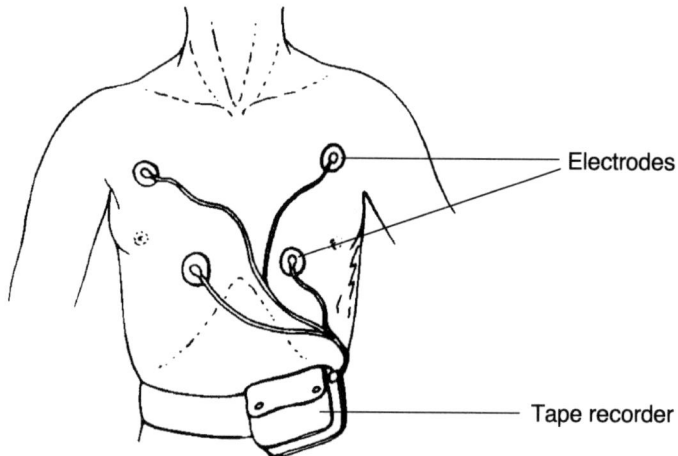

Figure 12. The arrangement for the 24 hour ECG tape recorder.

THE ECHOCARDIOGRAM

Echocardiography is undertaken by reflecting high-frequency sound waves (2–6mHz) from various interfaces of blood and muscle within the heart. The principle is the same as finding submarines under the sea. The most usual type of echo gives a two-dimensional picture which shows clear movement of the muscle and valves of the heart and can be recorded on a video tape (Figure 13). The technique is not easy and it may take an echocardiographer 10 years to become an expert. The value of the echocardiograph is in showing the structure of the heart as well as its function. It is painless and harmless and, whilst usually giving excellent pictures of the atria, ventricles and the four heart valves, cannot visualise the coronary arteries or any narrowing of them.

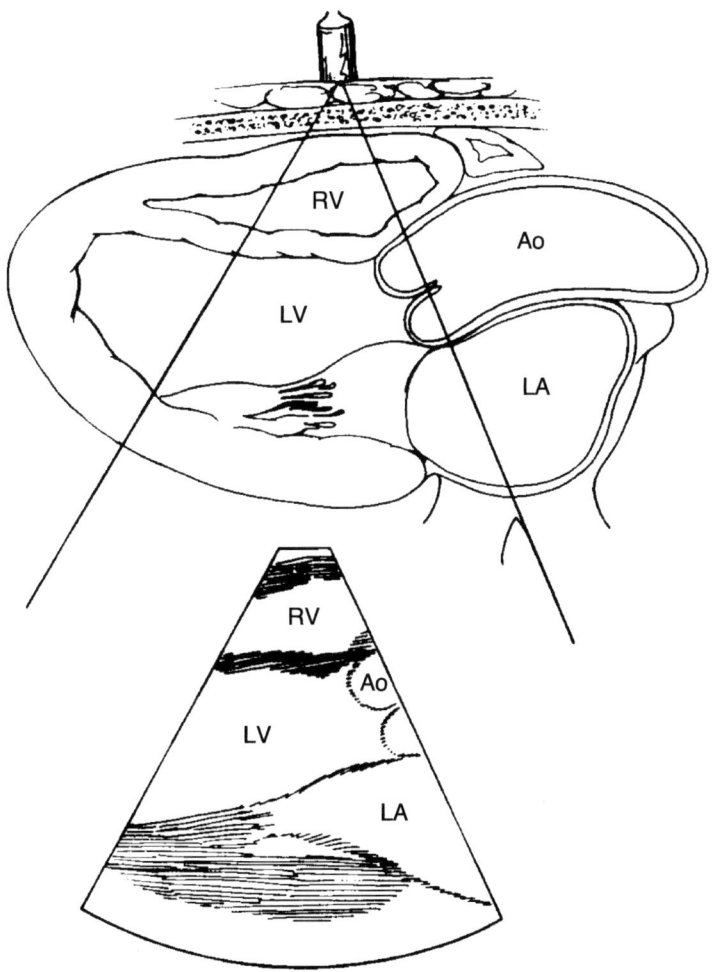

Figure 13. The two-dimensional echocardiograph. RV = right ventricle; LV = left ventricle; LA = left atrium; and Ao = aorta.

DOPPLER

A Doppler recording is usually done at the same time as echocardiography. The principle is to send sound waves across a moving stream of blood. The waves return to the transducer in a different pattern according to the speed of flow and turbulence within the blood vessel or heart (Figure 14, page 22). It is particularly useful in diagnosing the degree of narrowing or incompetence of heart valves. The same principle is used for measuring the narrowing of blood vessels such as the carotid and femoral arteries.

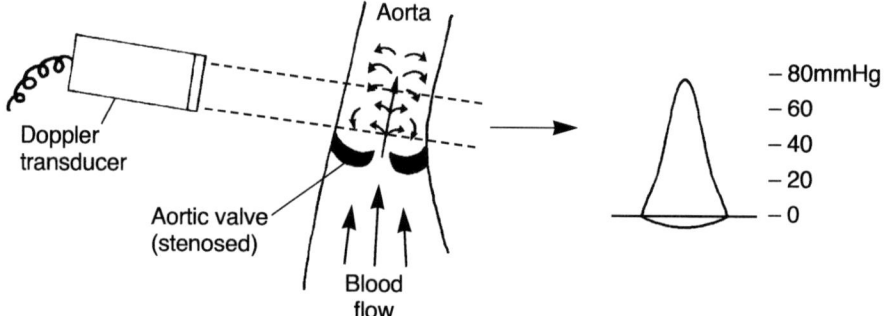

Figure 14. The principle of Doppler recording. The right hand chart shows how the gradient is measured.

CARDIAC CATHETERISATION

Cardiac catheterisation is generally regarded as the gold standard diagnostic test in cardiology. A catheter (a long, soft, plastic tube) is introduced via either the femoral artery or vein and, under X-ray control, is manoeuvred towards the heart. A catheter introduced into the femoral vein is manipulated successively into the inferior vena cava and possibly the superior vena cava, the right atrium, the right ventricle and the pulmonary artery.

The catheter introduced via the femoral artery is manipulated around the aorta through the aortic valve and into the left ventricle. Because of the shape of the heart and the sensitivity of the left ventricle for producing arrhythmias, it is not possible to get the left heart catheter into the left atrium. Specially shaped catheters are also introduced to enter the coronary arteries.

Although the femoral artery approach is the commonest, the catheter can also be introduced at the antecubital fossa into the brachial artery or vein. This requires a degree of dissection while entering the femoral artery or vein and can be performed simply by the insertion of a needle. If the femoral artery is difficult to locate because of obesity, or the patient has a severely narrowed femoral artery due to atheroma, it may be sensible to use the brachial artery approach which will be easier and safer (Figure 15).

The value of cardiac catheterisation is as follows.

Pressure measurements

Highly accurate pressure measurements can be made in all chambers of the heart except the left atrium. Special catheters can be introduced to the left atrium by piercing the atrial septum, although this is seldom required. Pressure gradients will give an exact estimate of the degree of valve stenosis.

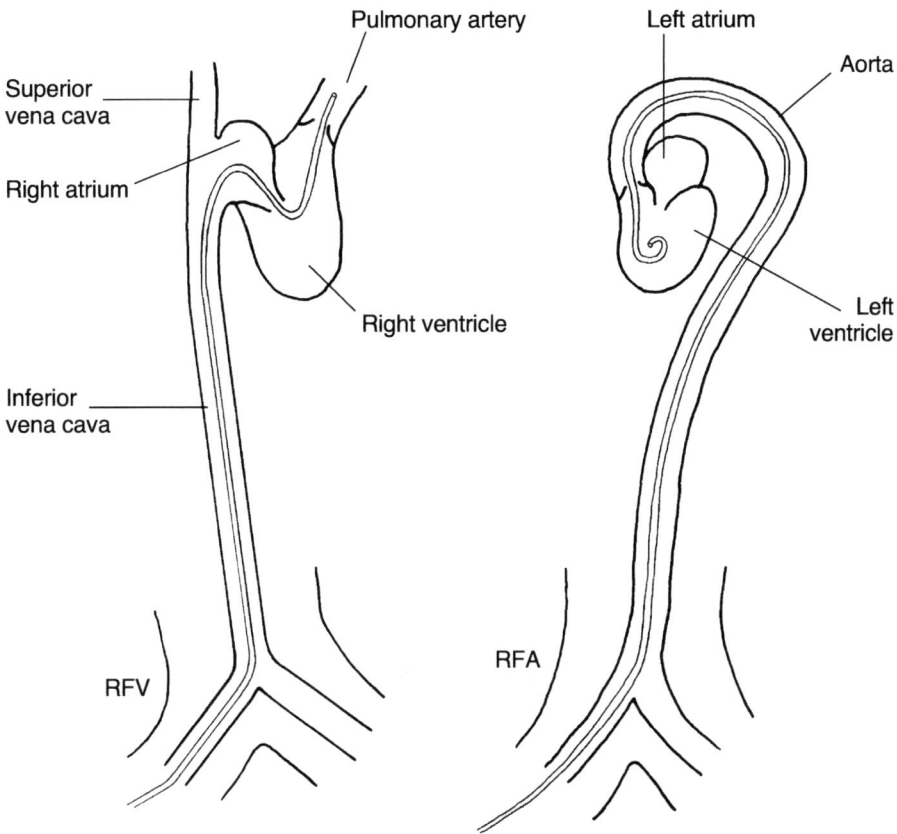

Figure 15. The right heart catheter (left) and the left heart catheter (right).

Angiography

The rapid introduction of contrast or dye into either the chambers of the heart or the coronary arteries will give an extremely accurate picture of the shape of the chambers or any possible narrowing of the coronary artery. The dye is iodine based and completely harmless, although in quantity can give a hot feeling for about 5sec as it circulates around the body. As the dye enters the heart, X-ray pictures are taken from several different directions in order to get an exact three-dimensional picture of the chamber or artery concerned.

Oxygen saturations

From various chambers of the heart, a small amount of blood can be withdrawn and its oxygen saturation measured. Blood should be 100% saturated with oxygen on the left side of the heart; when it returns to the heart via the vena cavae and into the right atrium and right ventricle, its saturation is usually about 70%. A shunt of blood from the left side of the heart to the right side, or vice versa, can occur because of a communication between the two halves of the heart, eg atrial septal defect or ventricular septal defect. This will cause oxygenated blood to be mixed with desaturated blood.

If, for example, there is a ventricular septal defect, blood will pass from the left ventricle directly to the right ventricle. There will be a step up, therefore, in oxygen saturation from the right atrium to the right ventricle in proportion to the amount of blood flowing from the left ventricle. Thus, the degree of shunt can be ascertained which will indicate the size of the defect and, more importantly, how much it is likely to affect the patient in later life. A large shunt will need closure or the patient will develop severe pulmonary hypertension in later years (Figure 16).

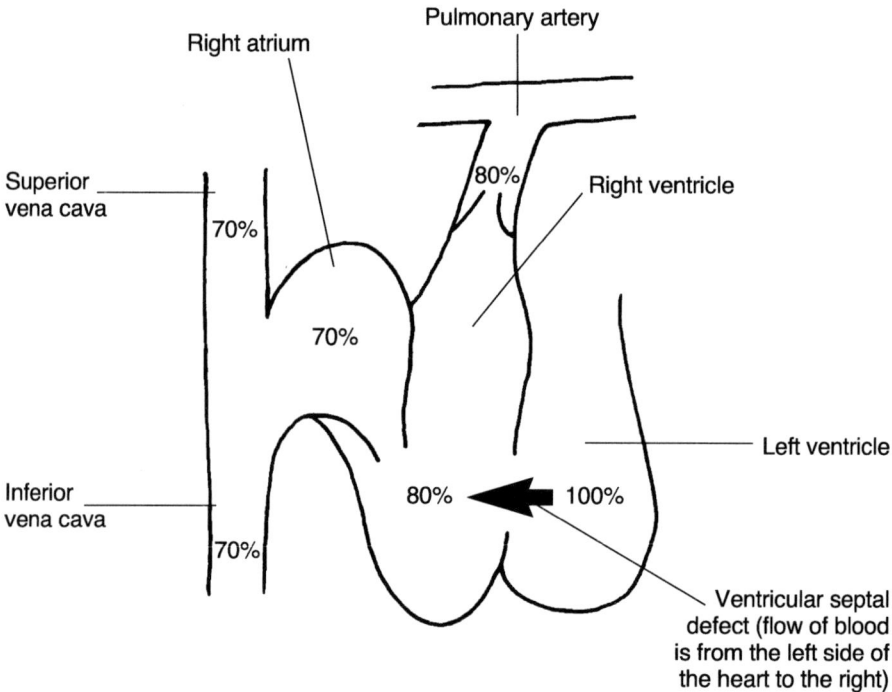

Figure 16. Oxygen saturations in a ventricular septal defect. Note the oxygen step-up at ventricular level.

The risks of cardiac catheterisation

There are risks of cardiac catheterisation. As with any invasive procedure on the body, there is some risk either to the blood vessel where the catheter is introduced or problems related to the heart itself. However, the overall risk of this procedure is very small (see Table 1).

Risk	%
Death	0.14
Embolus/stroke	0.12
Damage to femoral artery	1.70
Heart attack	0.07
Ventricular fibrillation	0.60

Table 1. Risks of cardiac catheterisation.

During the catheterisation the most frequent problem is of ventricular ectopic beats caused by the catheter stimulating the wall of the ventricle itself. Very rarely this could give rise to a ventricular tachycardia or ventricular fibrillation. The risk of death or a heart attack is very small indeed, and in any case is usually confined to those patients at high risk.

In order to prevent problems at the site of the arterial or venous puncture, considerable pressure is exerted at the end of the procedure at the site of the catheter insertion in the groin to prevent bleeding. Because of the close proximity of the femoral nerve, this can be uncomfortable. It is, however, worthwhile in view of the benefit obtained.

Damage to the femoral artery is possible even with the most experienced operator and is generally considered 'accidental'. The main reason for this is that the anatomy in the groin is variable and the artery may lie in front of the vein, or vice versa. Even though an operation may rarely be required to repair the femoral artery, the risks of the whole procedure are low.

ELECTROPHYSIOLOGY

Electrophysiological studies are performed in a manner similar to cardiac catheterisation. Instead of a catheter being introduced into the heart, a flexible, plastic-covered electrode is introduced into the chambers of the heart to record the intra-cardiac electrical activity. There are two basic functions of this technique. The first is to find evidence of heart block (see Chapter 11 on arrhythmias) where there is an interruption of electrical activity from the atria to the ventricles and down the bundle of His. Secondly one looks for the presence of an additional electrical pathway which competes with the bundle of His (see Chapters 1 on anatomy and 11) and is responsible for 'reciprocal' tachycardias.

Having mapped out the positions of the pathways, the patient may receive a pacemaker if her problem is a slow heart rate. If the problem is tachycardias, ablation of the extra bypass tract can be achieved by electric shock or other means. The risks of this procedure are very much the same as that for cardiac catheterisation.

ISOTOPE STUDIES

An isotope such as thallium-201 attached to a protein (eg albumin) is introduced into the body by an injection. After circulating it is taken up by heart tissue. In a typical isotope study thallium-201 is taken up by viable heart tissue but is not taken up by tissue which is dead or ischaemic. When a gamma camera then takes a picture, it shows a cold spot indicating the absence of thallium and hence an area of the heart which is either dead or potentially dying tissue.

There are now a large number of different types of isotope scans which are performed either to delineate dead tissue or potentially salvageable tissue which may be stunned or hibernating. The risks of this particular study are minimal because the radioactivity produced by the thallium is negligible. Sometimes isotope studies are taken before and after exercise on a treadmill. In addition, isotopes circulating in the blood can demonstrate the left ventricular stroke volume.

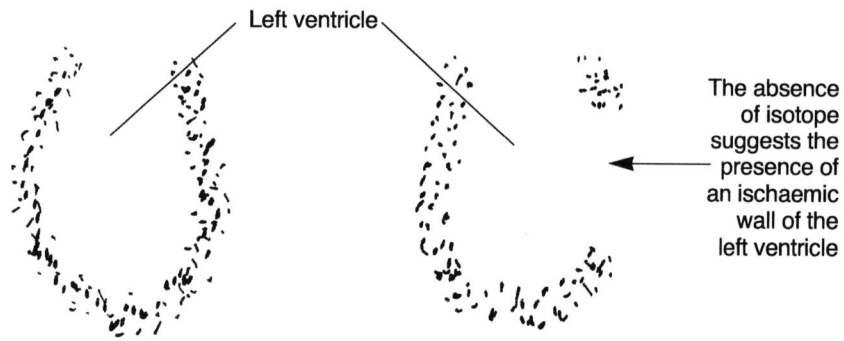

Figure 17. Isotope scanning before exercise (left) and after exercise (right).

CT AND MRI SCANS

These scans are of limited value for the heart because it is a moving object. If the heart were to stay still for a while it might even be possible to see the coronary arteries without cardiac catheterisation. As this is not possible, the value of the scan is limited to looking at the overall structure of the heart and an assessment of left ventricular function.

The basis of the CT scan is to take X-ray pictures at angles all round the body and then to create a two-dimensional image of the heart using computers.

The newer type of scan is called a magnetic resonance imaging (MRI) scan, which works on a completely different principle. Because of this it has more potential than a CT scan, although its full value will not be realised for some years. The principle of the MRI scan is that ions (eg hydrogen ions) line up at a particular angle within the cell when a strong magnetic current is put through the body (Figure 18). When the magnetic current is switched off, the ions move back to their original position and in doing so release a radio wave. This particular wave is then picked up by the scanning machine. Structures containing very little water, eg bone, will produce fewer radio waves, whereas blood, which is largely water, will produce a strong picture. The scan, therefore, is black and white with all shades of grey in between. The value of MRI scanning is greater when it distinguishes between dying and living tissue.

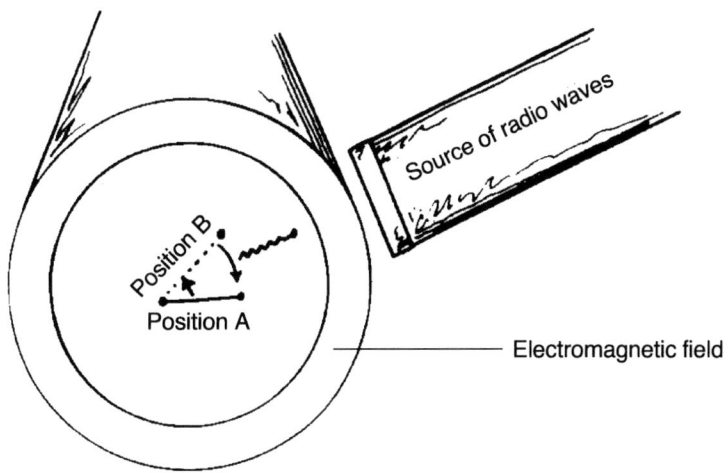

Figure 18. The principle of nuclear magnetic resonance imaging. Any hydrogen ions in living tissue will line up in a particular plane. When bombarded with radio waves this plane will shift through a certain number of degrees. When the radio wave source is switched off, the hydrogen ions return to their original plane and release a burst of radio waves which can be recorded by the transducer.

CHAPTER FOUR

ATHEROMA

INTRODUCTION

Atheroma is derived from the Greek word for porridge, and because it causes by far the most heart disease in any Western country it deserves some expansion on its cause and underlying risk factors. It is not entirely clear whether atheroma was present in the last century because post-mortems then were not done to the standards of today, and in any case people died at a much earlier age due to infection. The dramatic increase in heart attacks in the 1920s and subsequently through to the present day has suggested that it is an epidemic which has hit the world in the 20th century.

It must be clearly emphasised that we do not know the cause of atheroma and how it comes to be laid down in the arteries. Atheroma itself consists of cholesterol and other fats along with a variety of different types of cell and scar tissue. Overlying the atheroma is a layer of epithelium which normally allows blood to pass over it without clotting.

THE BLOOD VESSELS INVOLVED

Atheroma seems to have a prediliction for certain blood vessels and in the majority of cases accumulates in the coronary arteries prior to other arteries. The carotid arteries may also show evidence of atheroma which may lead to a stroke and if the femoral arteries become narrowed, it causes intermittent claudication, ie pains in the calves, especially on walking. The process of atheroma is usually very slow. It is possible to show flecks of atheroma in children as young as three years, and it is common to find obvious plaques in teenage years. Gradual narrowing then appears to occur over a long period of time, typically 40 years, until the narrowing becomes critical and begins to affect blood flow, especially with exercise.

Atheroma is not like the furring up of water pipes. Narrowing occurs over a discrete distance, usually of about 1cm. Long narrowed lesions may occur which are difficult to deal with surgically or by angioplasty. Generally speaking, the younger the patient the softer the atheroma. In later life atheroma will become calcified when the underlying scar tissue makes the lesion difficult to manipulate by angioplasty.

A heart attack occurs when a clot develops at the site of a narrowing. Precisely why this should happen is not known. It is possible that the atheromatous plaque splits and the underlying tissue which is not covered by epithelium allows a clot to form. It is also possible that local spasm of the coronary artery around the narrowing causes the atheroma to block the artery completely so that a clot might form.

In unstable angina it is thought that some episodes of pain are caused by platelet emboli. Platelets are the building blocks of clots whilst clotting factors provide the cement which keeps them tightly together. Fortunately platelet emboli are easily dispersed by the flow of the blood stream, and their occurrence is largely prevented by taking a small amount of aspirin each day.

RISK FACTORS

When considering risk factors it is important to make sure that there is a proper causal link. For example, in the 1950s the rise in the incidence of heart attacks exactly paralleled the rise in the purchase of television licences. Many risk factors have been suggested and it is considered at the moment that there may be as many as 256 independent risk factors for coronary heart disease. Only a few of these would be regarded as definitely significant, and only some of these are preventable.

Smoking

Smoking cigarettes is probably the most significant risk factor of all. Even smoking a few cigarettes increases the risk of heart disease, but the risk becomes very serious once somebody is smoking about 40 per day. If a male of 50 has smoked 40 cigarettes a day since he was a teenager, one can virtually guarantee him a heart attack. Cigarette smoking is basically an acidic form of smoking whereas cigar smoking is alkaline and appears to have no effect on coronary heart disease, though cigarette smoking and cigar smoking may have quite nasty effects upon the respiratory tract. Low tar cigarette smoking is no better than high tar smoking and even passive smoking is shown to be a significant factor.

In the US the percentage of people smoking has dropped over the last 20 years, but in this country it has changed very little with about 40% of the population smoking at some stage. Giving up smoking is of considerable benefit, dropping rapidly in the first couple of years following cessation of smoking, although the actual risk of heart disease never becomes completely normal, although it certainly moves towards it and more than justifies the efforts of giving up.

High blood fats

There are many fats which circulate around the body, the most important of which is cholesterol, which is divided, *inter alia*, into high density and low density lipoprotein (HDL and LDL). HDL is beneficial and helps to reduce the size of atheromatous plaques whilst LDL helps cholesterol accumulate in plaques much more readily. Therefore, quoting an overall figure for the presence of cholesterol can be at times be misleading, and a proper cholesterol result is only relevant if it is fractionated into HDL and LDL. Small quantities of HDL are far more effective than LDL and, as a rough guide, one should multiply the HDL by four to get a comparative amount with the LDL.

The cholesterol in the blood stream is about 20% derived from the diet, the rest is made by the liver. One must remember that cholesterol is vital to the body because the lining of every cell is made in part with cholesterol. Clearly, therefore, to lower cholesterol excessively may be hazardous. It is seldom possible to drop one's own cholesterol by more than about 20% simply by going on a low cholesterol diet. Extreme diets may lower the cholesterol by 30%, but rarely more. Consequently, if a patient has a very high cholesterol level, the only way of lowering it is some form of medication.

Until relatively recently this was a difficult task because existing drugs only lower cholesterol levels by 20%. However, recent drugs called statins have been far more effective and may lower the cholesterol by as much as 50%. Recent trial work has shown that not only the cholesterol drops with statins, but there is a clear benefit in terms of a reduction in mortality and cardiac events (eg heart attacks). Although statins can upset liver function tests, they usually return to normal when the drug is stopped.

There seem to be few if any long term side effects of the statins. It is important to note that the results of trials refer mainly to secondary prevention, ie after some form of cardiac episode has occurred. Proving primary prevention with statins is difficult although a recent Scottish trial was encouraging in this direction. Therefore, probably all people with very high cholesterol levels should be considered for statin treatment, especially if they have other risk factors.

The other lipids normally measured are the triglycerides, which are an independent risk factor for heart disease but much less significant than cholesterol. Triglyceride levels can usually be brought down by diet and reduction of alcohol. LDL is mainly reduced by diet and statins, whilst HDL is increased by exercise and small quantities of alcohol (2–4 units daily).

High blood pressure

The mechanism by which high blood pressure produces atheroma is not known. It is possible that blood pressure causes cracks in the lining of the coronary arteries which are then protected by the laying down of cholesterol. However, other than being aware that the control of blood pressure is important in atheroma, it is difficult to say more about aetiology.

Control of blood pressure is important, not only because of potential atheromatous development, but also because heart muscle will increase in size and outgrow its blood supply. Eventually the left ventricle will become dilated and weak with subsequent cardiac failure. The control and problems of blood pressure will be dealt with in another chapter.

Exercise

There is little doubt that exercise is beneficial to the body, but there is no clear proof that lack of exercise promotes the development of atheroma nor is there proof that vigorous exercise prevents the onset of atheroma. Exercise can certainly help to bring down blood pressure to a modest extent, which in turn can help to prevent atheroma. And it has been shown that moderate exercise such as brisk walking is as good as running long distances. Current advice is that one should exercise four or five times per week making oneself sufficiently breathless. This could be achieved by walking one mile briskly, ie in 15 minutes.

Obesity

There seems to be a general belief that obesity is one of the major factors in heart disease. Whilst obesity puts a greater strain upon the heart, there is no evidence that it increases mortality due to heart disease until you are 20–30% over your ideal body weight. It is sensible to keep your weight under control for a large number of reasons, but it is not correct to assume that if you are obese, you are automatically laying down cholesterol in your arteries.

Stress

Like obesity, stress is regarded as perhaps the major risk factor for heart disease in the general population. Again this is not true, and the proof that stress is a major risk factor is lacking. There is little doubt that there is a higher incidence of heart attacks after a major life crisis such as the death of a loved one, divorce or an unwanted retirement, but background stress that affects everyday life has not been shown to be a clear factor in the promotion of atheroma. Because stress is not measurable and because everybody responds differently to stress to some degree, it is very difficult to prove the association between stress and atheroma.

Others

Other factors such as the hardness of water and the lack of selenium in the diet have all been shown to have some minor correlation with ischaemic heart disease. However, the association is relatively trivial and certainly could not be regarded as a significant factor that needs to be altered in everyday life.

CHAPTER FIVE

ANGINA PECTORIS AND UNSTABLE ANGINA

ANGINA PECTORIS

Introduction

Angina (strangle) pectoris (chest) was first described before it was believed the heart could be responsible for any sort of illness within the body. It is thus a description of clinical symptoms, first described by Heberden in 1768. In its nature it is unchanged today. Angina pectoris refers to pain coming on in the chest, radiating to the arms (usually left) or neck, and associated with exercise or excitement. It is relieved when the stimulus ceases. It is worse in cold or windy weather or after a large meal when the heart's cardiac output increases.

It is important to be aware that this is the correct description of angina and that the word angina does not refer to just any pain in the chest which may or may not be associated with the heart. It must also be noted that angina does not refer to any other symptoms such as breathlessness or tiredness.

Pathophysiology

The vast majority of patients with angina have narrowed coronary arteries. This causes a restriction of the flow of blood into the heart muscle as the patient exercises. Thus the supply of blood does not keep up with demand and the patient perceives pain in the chest. This pain is a protective mechanism preventing the patient from over-exertion and is not indicative of damage occurring to the heart.

Angina is very variable from one day to the next due to factors which are not fully understood. One day a person may be able to walk 400 yards before getting angina and the next day only 50 yards, despite the presence of similar conditions. This variability is probably due to the muscle tone of the artery. An artery is rather like a piece of rubber tubing made of muscle. If the muscle constricts, the size of the lumen inside the artery will be decreased and this will clearly worsen the degree of angina.

Occasionally angina can occur in the presence of normal coronary arteries. The mechanism of angina in this case is not known and it is termed 'syndrome X'. Because it is common in menopausal females, it was unfortunately thought to be of neurotic origin. However, there is little doubt that it is a genuine clinical entity and it is either related to restriction within tiny blood vessels which cannot be seen on angiograms, etc, or a cellular problem due to the inability of the cell to provide sufficient energy. Nevertheless the treatment of syndrome X is very similar to that of ordinary angina.

The diagnosis of angina

The diagnosis of angina is made on the patient's history. The old adage in medicine which says 'listen to the patient, he is telling you the diagnosis' is especially relevant to angina. If, after taking a history, there is uncertainty about the diagnosis of angina, physical signs will seldom be present and helpful. High blood pressure is a risk factor of ischaemic heart disease and one may find heart murmurs or extra sounds which indicate heart failure. This would only indicate the presence of heart disease and not the presence of angina. Other risk factors may be helpful in the diagnosis, eg smoking, being male, post-menopausal or diabetic, high blood lipids, a positive family history, obesity and stress.

If the diagnosis is not clear from history and examination, an ECG should be carried out and subsequently an exercise test. The resting ECG is of limited value and is frequently normal. The exercise test, however, is much more helpful. For example, there are a number of ECG changes occurring with exercise which indicate the presence of an impaired blood supply of the heart and thus ischaemic heart disease.

The value of the exercise test is not only diagnostic; it is also prognostic. A test which is strongly positive, eg with angina or changes on the ECG occurring after 1–2 minutes walking, may indicate quite severe or critical heart disease that needs further urgent investigation. A strongly positive test may indicate left main stem disease which is known as the 'widow-maker' because of its high incidence of sudden death (Figure 19). A narrowing of the first part

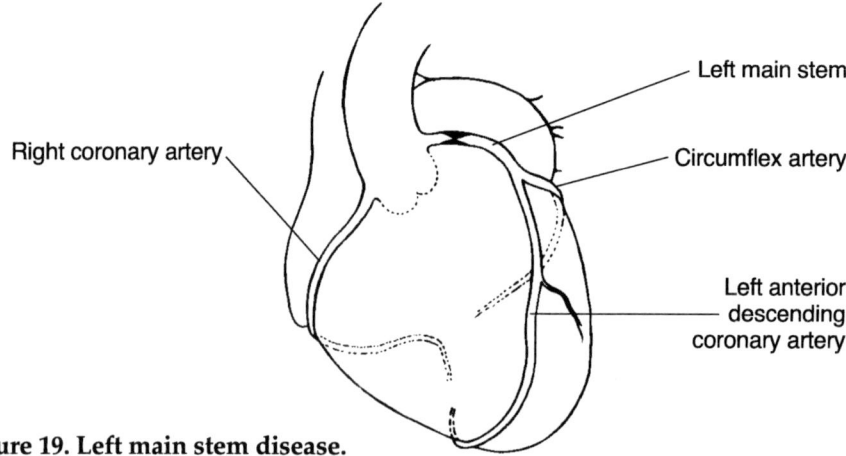

Figure 19. Left main stem disease.

of the left coronary artery near its origin jeopardises a large area of heart muscle. These patients have an improved life expectancy after bypass grafting and must be identified as early as possible.

Treatment of angina

The treatment of angina can be medical and surgical.

Medical treatment

Medical treatment consists of anti-anginal medication and the elimination of risk factors, especially smoking, which can significantly influence the long term course of angina. There are three main types of medication (and now possibly a fourth) which are generally used in this condition, and the order of their use depends on the doctor's preference.

(a) Beta-blockers (eg Bisoprolol, Atenolol, Propranolol)

These tablets reduce both the force of contraction of the heart and the heart rate itself. In doing so they reduce the demand by the heart for oxygen supply. They are highly effective drugs and probably the most powerful of all those available for angina. The problems of beta-blockers are their side effects. The catch phrase for them is 'weariness and dreariness'. In addition they can provoke asthma in a susceptible patient and, although some beta-blockers are said to be cardio-selective, all of them must be totally precluded in patients who have an asthmatic tendency.

Because beta-blockers vaso-constrict the blood vessels of the skin, patients may complain of cold hands and feet. This is seldom worrying although very inconvenient, but can cause problems to patients with restricted blood flow to their legs and may worsen intermittent claudication. The beta-blockers first produced in the 1960s generally have more side effects compared with the more later generations of beta-blockers. It is possible, therefore, to have a beta-blocker which does not produce quite such a degree of fatigue, etc, but all beta-blockers will do this to some degree.

(b) Calcium antagonists (eg Verapamil, Diltiazem, Amlodopine)

Whilst it is known that these tablets affect the calcium metabolism within the cell and block some of its activity, it is not really known exactly how they work. What they do is to uncouple electrical and mechanical contraction and thus reduce the amount of energy required within the cell. This in turn reduces the necessity of the blood supply and keeps demand down. They work well with beta-blockers and, because they work in a different way, are additive. The only calcium antagonist which should not be used with a beta-blocker is Verapamil. The side effects of calcium antagonists tend to be related to their vasodilating effect. If they vasodilate the main arteries too much, the patient may feel light headed and dizzy and experience flushing of the face. If the peripheral arterioles vasodilate, the patient's skin may become red, especially the legs; ankle oedema may also develop. The calcium antagonists are probably second to beta-blockers in their ability to control angina.

(c) Nitrates (eg dinitrates, mononitrates, glyceryl trinitrate)

Nitrates are usually used in the form of a tablet or spray under the tongue, enabling very rapid absorption. Their action is to dilate arteries. During angina the coronary arteries are maximally dilated because of the lack of oxygen, and nitrates work by dilating the blood vessels of the general circulation, making the work of the heart easier and therefore reducing the demand for oxygen. Nitrate under the tongue acts within 2–3 minutes and remains effective for about 30 minutes.

Long acting nitrates such as the mononitrates taken orally seem to be effective over a longer period of time. The principal side effect of nitrates is the dilatation of blood vessels in the brain leading to headache. Occasionally excessive dilatation of blood vessels can cause a lowering of blood pressure and subsequent fainting.

(d) Potassium channel openers

A fourth class of drugs, potassium channel openers, has recently become available and may add a new group of drugs to existing medication.

Patients are usually started on one type of anti-anginal therapy and increased gradually to triple therapy according to the degree of control of their angina.

Surgical treatment

There are two forms of surgical treatment possible: angioplasty and coronary artery bypass grafting.

(a) Angioplasty

Angioplasty is the principle of introducing a catheter with a small balloon on its end into a coronary artery. The balloon is inflated across a narrowing and forces the atheromatous material into the lining of the artery (Figure 20). This pre-supposes that the atheroma is soft. In elderly patients the atheroma may be so rigid and calcified that this procedure may not be possible.

Angioplasty was first introduced in about 1978 and is therefore a relatively new procedure. It cannot be used for every narrowing of the coronary arteries. Its prime use is for one or two vessel disease where the narrowing is quite close to the origin of the artery, which means it is technically possible to cross it and obliterate the atheroma.

The balloon is inflated with carbon dioxide to five atmospheres pressure for approximately 30 seconds. If the balloon is left inflated too long, the blockage of the coronary artery might result in a heart attack. The balloon is repeatedly inflated across the narrowing until the doctor is satisfied that he

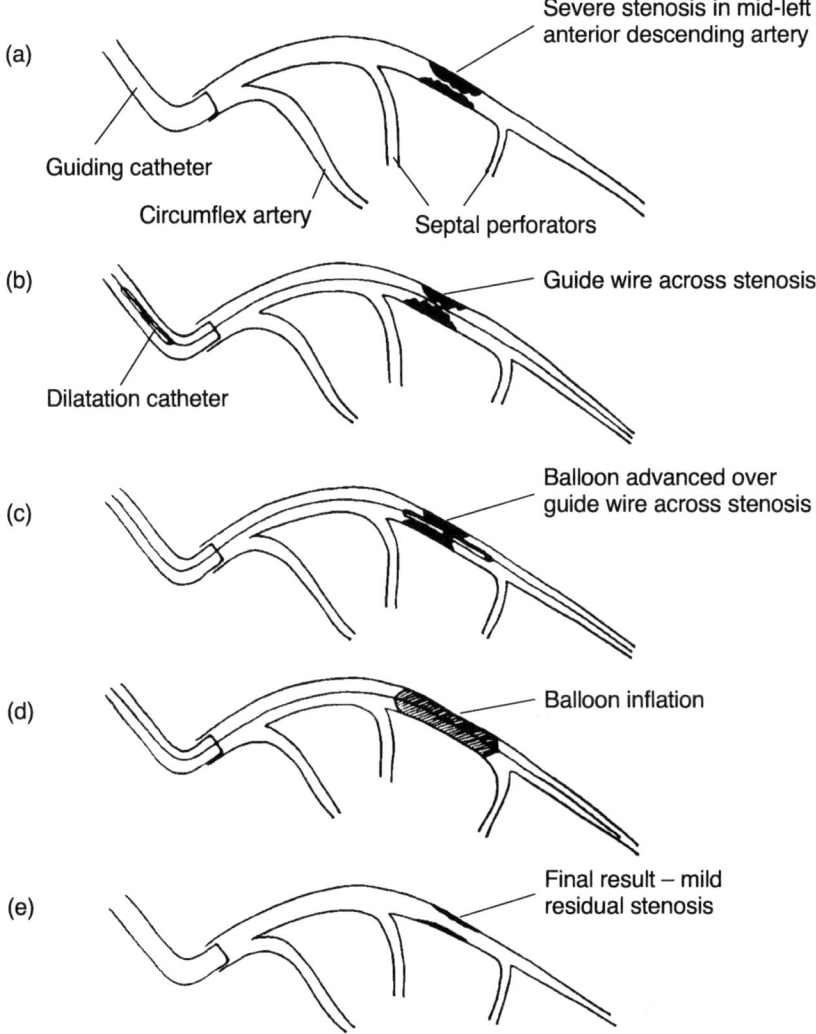

Figure 20. The principle of coronary angioplasty and the stages involved:

(a) the guiding catheter is positioned in the ostium of the left coronary artery – angiography shows a severe stenosis in the mid-anterior descending artery;

(b) a guide wire (0.014–0.018in diameter) is positioned across the stenosis, with the balloon catheter (dilatation catheter) remaining in the shaft of the guiding catheter;

(c) the dilatation catheter is advanced across the stenosis;

(d) the balloon is inflated; and

(e) the balloon and guide wire are withdrawn for the final angiogram.

has obliterated as much of the narrowing as possible. If the wall of the artery appears to be slightly ragged or even split, it is possible to put a stent inside the artery to prevent it collapsing. A stent is a small metal tube (0.5–1in long) made like wire mesh and which fits snugly into the artery. This procedure is being increasingly used and in experienced hands is very good. The problem of putting a stent into the coronary artery is that it predisposes towards clotting in the early stages after insertion, and therefore the patient must be anticoagulated for three months from the time of the angioplasty.

Approximately 75% of those people who have angioplasty will only need the procedure performed once. The remaining 25% would usually get a recurrence of the narrowing (for reasons which are uncertain) within the first month or so and will need redilating. After either one or two angioplasty procedures, the success rate approaches 95% (relief of angina). It is still uncertain how long angioplasties remain beneficial and a recent major study suggested that after 18 months approximately 50% of patients experience some angina again, albeit often mild. The angioplasty can, of course, can be repeated at this stage and many times through life.

About 3% of patients, usually those who are older and with more critical lesions, will require emergency coronary artery bypass grafting. Patient must be warned of this before they have angioplasty. Nevertheless, the procedure of angioplasty usually saves the patient having to have an operation and is relatively easily performed under local anaesthetic. The success rate is generally high and the patient can be back at work within two days. It is normal for patients to be discharged on warfarin if a stent has been inserted, and otherwise aspirin and Diltiazem for three months.

(b) Coronary artery bypass grafting

The level of expertise of this operation in this country is now considerable. A bypass conduit takes blood from the aorta to a point distal to the narrowing on the coronary artery, thus restoring flow to the distal part of the vessel concerned. This is the coronary artery vein graft. The saphenous vein is exposed and with great care is dissected and removed, reversed in direction (it contains valves) and inserted as appropriate (Figure 21).

Many patients may also have a left (and occasionally right) internal mammary artery bypass graft. This particular artery in the thorax is 'spare' and can be mobilised and placed into the left anterior descending coronary artery. Because it is an artery its patency rates are very high and it is particularly useful as an additional type of bypass graft.

Generally speaking, if it is possible to use this particular artery then the procedure is performed. The patient who has bypass grafting remains in hospital for 7–10 days. He recovers quite rapidly after the operation and feels initially very cheerful, but may succumb to a temporary depression for a few days. After going home the patient mobilises slowly and returns to work after

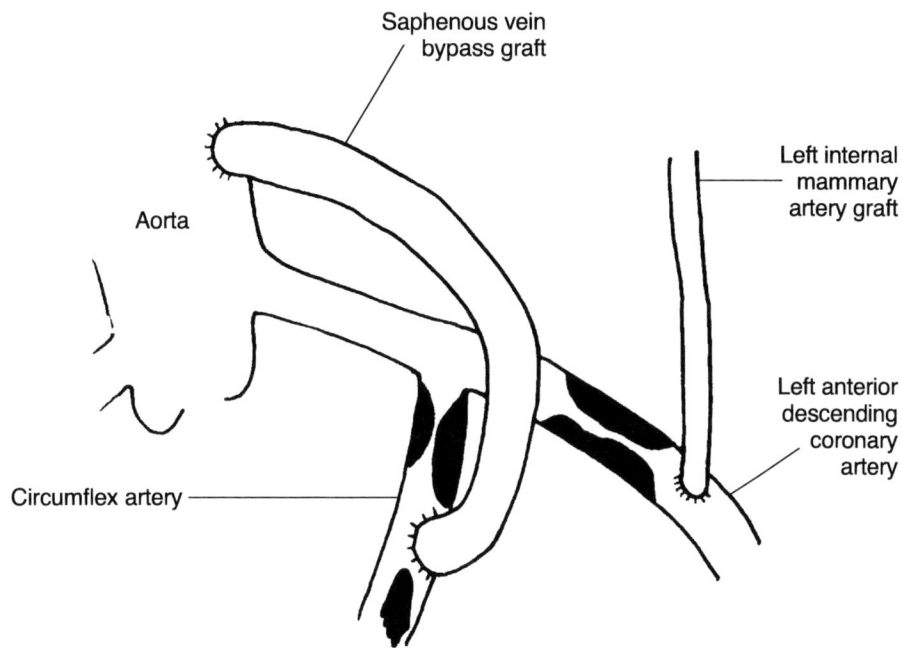

Figure 21. Bypass grafting of the coronary artery.

between six weeks and three months. The success rate of the operation is over 90%, and its overwhelming function is to relieve chest pain.

It is not an operation which specifically helps breathlessness or tiredness, although this may happen. In two circumstances there is a definite benefit in life expectancy. The five year mortality from left main stem disease treated medically is 40%, whilst the surgical mortality at five years is 10%. With triple vessel disease, the five year mortality medically is 20% and the five year mortality surgically is 10%.

The patency of the coronary arteries is variable, but they may last many years. There seems to be a general belief that coronary artery bypass grafting lasts for only 10 years. This is not so, and the length of time the operation is of value varies but can be many years.

(c) Indications for an angiogram and subsequent surgical intervention

The main reason to operate upon a patient is failed medical therapy, which comes in two forms. In the first and more obvious type the patient still has significant chest pain despite maximum medical therapy. The other form of failed medical therapy is where medical treatment may be reducing the chest pain sufficiently, but only at the expense of such significant side effects that the quality of life becomes unacceptable. If, for example, a 50 year old man has little pain but feels permanently 'weary and dreary' and has impotence as a result of his drugs, it is reasonable to consider either angioplasty or an operation.

The mortality rate in performing angioplasty is approximately 0.5%, and the mortality in performing bypass grafting is approximately 1%. There is no official age limit for coronary artery bypass grafting, although in a patient with a biological age greater than 75, angioplasty would be performed if at all possible. After bypass grafting, rehabilitation is very important and provided by many hospitals in this country. During this time it is also particularly important to eliminate any risk factors, especially smoking.

The future

Various types of cutting devices have been tried as an alternative to angioplasty and some of these may develop into useful techniques. Included in this is laser treatment. The problem is that, whilst it is easy for a laser to create passages through atheroma, it is equally easy for it to damage the artery wall because direct vision is impossible in coronary arteries at the present time.

More recently there have been attempts to improve the circulation within ischaemic tissue by making multiple laser holes in the myocardium. This is not yet a validated technique, but is something that may be tried when all else fails. Trans-thoracic epidural stimulation has been tried, but this technique relieves pain and has little effect on the underlying heart disease.

UNSTABLE ANGINA

Introduction

Unstable angina is a serious condition and is effectively half way between typical angina and myocardial infarction. There is no single definition of unstable angina, but it may come into the following categories:

(a) ordinary angina increasing in severity over a matter of a few weeks; eg a patient may be able to walk half a mile comfortably with his angina, but three weeks later can only manage 50 yards;

(b) angina of an ordinary nature suddenly becoming intermingled with chest pain at rest; and

(c) episodes of anginal pain chest pain which seem typical of a myocardial infarction but, after investigation, are found not to indicate damage of heart tissue. Such pains usually last 10–20 minutes instead of perhaps the 30–60 minutes which one would normally associate with a myocardial infarction.

Pathophysiology

It is not known what causes unstable angina. However, small clots of platelets which break up relatively easily are thought to be the most likely cause, especially as aspirin and other anti-platelet agents have a beneficial effect upon the subsequent incidence of myocardial infarction and death.

Management

Initially, medical management is the treatment of choice. The most important drugs involved are heparin and aspirin. Subcutaneous heparin can reduce the mortality and incidence of heart attack in this condition by 70–90%. Reduction of mortality by aspirin alone is probably about 40–50%, but the effects of heparin and aspirin together do not seem to be additive.

So far trials using thrombolysis (drugs which dissolve clots) have not shown any benefit in unstable angina but this may change. Beta-blockers may be given in unstable angina and appear to offer a 10–15% reduction in mortality and morbidity. Other tablets which are used, such as calcium antagonists and nitrates, appear to have little effect upon mortality and morbidity at all. Nitrates are frequently used in unstable angina because they have a very beneficial effect upon chest pain. This is usually achieved by a nitrate infusion which is gradually reduced as the pain decreases.

With this medical regime, 85% of patients will settle and will be discharged from hospital. However, all of them should be followed up with coronary angiography with or without preceding exercise testing. It is dangerous to exercise a patient in the acute phase of unstable angina because one may provoke a cardiac arrest.

In approximately 15% of occasions medical treatment does not settle unstable angina. If pains become recurrent the patient will undoubtedly require angiography. Thus, during admission for unstable angina transfer to a teaching or tertiary hospital may be necessary. Angiography will delineate the lesion, often a 90% narrowing, which is most likely to be causing the unstable angina. After angiography, a decision is made as to whether to proceed to angioplasty or coronary artery bypass grafting. The success of these procedures is similar to stable angina although results may be modified by the extent of left ventricular damage occurring prior to the current episode.

CHAPTER SIX

MYOCARDIAL INFARCTION

INTRODUCTION

Myocardial infarction is the complete blockage of one of the three main coronary arteries. A blockage will occur at the site of a narrowing and, unlike unstable angina, the blockage will be permanent unless active intervention is made. In the 1950s most patients were kept at home because there was no treatment other than pain relief for heart attacks. Those who were admitted to hospital were put on strict bed rest for six weeks and were almost unable to move a muscle. Mortality was about 40%, much of which was due to clots forming because of immobility. The remaining patients died, it was thought, from heart muscle failure.

In about 1960 in the UK and USA it was discovered that the electrical activity of the heart was abnormal immediately after a heart attack. Abnormal rhythms followed by ventricular fibrillation caused cardiac arrest. Coronary care units were set up to monitor these problems and, with the advent of anti-arrhythmic drugs, the mortality dropped dramatically to 20%. Other drug developments for arrhythmias and heart muscle as well as open heart surgery saw a gradual decline in the mortality of heart attacks to about 12% in the 1980s. The advent of thrombolysis has now reduced this to as little as 6% (Figure 22).

Although most patients who have a heart attack are sent to hospital, it is not always necessary. Very elderly patients, those severely ill with other diseases or those whose pain has been present for several days before they present, may have little to gain by going into hospital.

IMMEDIATE HOME MANAGEMENT

A classic coronary will present with severe central chest pain associated with pallor and sweating. This will make the diagnosis relatively easy. If the GP is called to see a patient such as this he will usually have knowledge of the background of the patient (eg heavy smoker) and may, therefore, be able to make the diagnosis within a matter of seconds. However, many myocardial infarctions present with a range of pain from little or none to very severe, and the GP must take a careful history from the patient as well as examine him and note any risk factors.

If he considers that the patient has had an acute myocardial infarction, his first action must be to give the patient an aspirin which should be chewed and swallowed quickly. This acts as a thrombolysing agent to dissolve the clot. His second action will be to summon help in the form of an ambulance. This may have already been done as many modern protocols include alerting an ambulance at the same time as a doctor is called to a patient with significant chest pain. If an ambulance has not been called, the patient's spouse or another person would have to help the doctor. Thirdly the doctor must afford pain relief. This should be done with morphine or one of its analogues which gives considerable relief of pain and a feeling of well being. Most ambulances will be with the patient within 10–20 minutes and it is the doctor's responsibility to wait with the patient until the ambulance arrives, although it is not necessary for the doctor to accompany the patient to hospital.

Modern trials do not indicate that thrombolysis has a significant benefit if given by the GP at home unless the hospital is a long way from the patient's house. It is unlikely, therefore, that in the next few years we shall see streptokinase or other thrombolytic agent being given at home. There has been a suggestion that all GPs should have a defibrillator. Calculating from major trials, a GP would probably have to deal with one cardiac arrest every three years, and it does not seem justified for him to have a defibrillator for this rare occasion, especially when all resuscitative equipment arrives with the ambulance. The GP is expected to give adequate cardio-pulmonary resuscitation if necessary.

The diagnosis of chest pains at home are notoriously difficult and will inevitably lead to a number of medico-legal cases. Failure to diagnose a myocardial infarction may cause great distress.

IMMEDIATE HOSPITAL MANAGEMENT

The Casualty Officer or medical SHO would probably have been warned that a coronary is on its way by the ambulance crew. As soon as the patient with chest pain arrives, an ECG is performed and a decision made regarding thrombolysis. Because chest pains in casualty are such a common occurrence, doctors at all levels should be able to interpret the ECG in myocardial ischaemia. These commonly include Q-waves, ST segment elevation or depression and T-wave flattening or inversion (Figure 23). However, in the early stages of a myocardial infarction there may be no signs on the ECG. This does not exclude the diagnosis of myocardial infarction.

The earliest changes of a myocardial infarction normally happen within half an hour, with ST segment elevation being the first sign on the ECG followed by T-wave inversion and subsequently Q-waves. Once a diagnosis of probable myocardial infarction is made, thrombolysis must be instituted as fast as possible. If aspirin has not been given at the patient's home, it must be given immediately, followed by streptokinase or tissue plasminogen activator (tPA). Streptokinase is a 90 minute infusion whereas tPA can be given as a rapid single dose injection. While the latter may be preferable, it costs approximately £600 compared with £80 for streptokinase. Because there is no practical difference between streptokinase and tPA, streptokinase is normally used in the UK except when contraindicated.

The effect of thrombolysis is to restore blood flow to an area of tissue which is being jeopardised. Within this tissue there will be areas where myocardium has been injured and there will be a change of biochemical functions within the cell. As a result of the sudden restoration of oxygen to the cell, its functions may become temporarily disorganised and arrhythmias may occur. During thrombolysis, therefore, and immediately afterwards, a patient

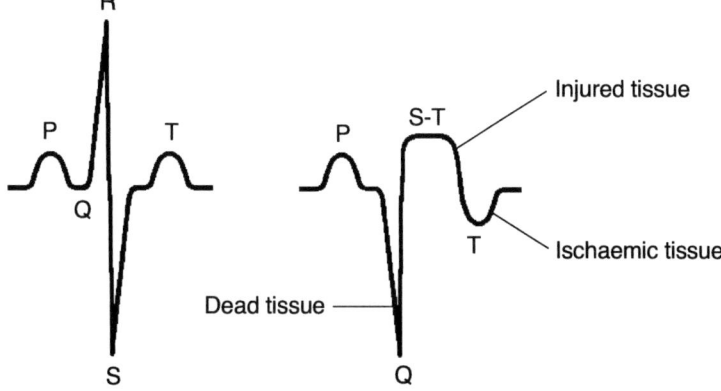

Figure 23. A normal ECG (left) and an ECG of myocardial infarction (right).

must be carefully monitored. Ventricular fibrillation is possible during this period which is one of the reasons why streptokinase is not readily given in the patient's home.

In addition to thrombolysis, pain-relief must be given if necessary, and blood will normally be taken for the measurement of cardiac enzymes, electrolytes including potassium, a full blood count to detect anaemia and a plasma glucose. In any stress reaction the blood glucose will rise, although a myocardial infarction may be the first presentation of a diabetic.

THROMBOLYSIS

Thrombolysis is the biggest single advance in the treatment of myocardial infarction since the advent of coronary care units in 1960. The benefit of thrombolysis depends on the speed at which it is given following the occlusion of the coronary artery. In general terms the mortality reduction within the first hour may be as high at 50%, within six hours 25%, within 12 hours 12% and within 24 hours about 6%. Since the latter is not statistically

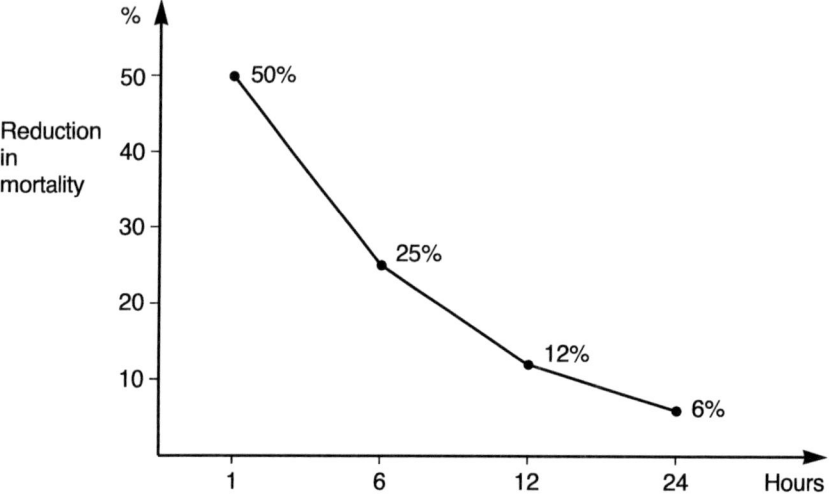

Figure 22. Approximate reduction in mortality using thrombolysis for myocardial infarction.

significant, most hospitals give thrombolysis only up to 12 hours.

Because the effects of thrombolysis are to dissolve any clot in the body, care must be taken if there are potential bleeding sites elsewhere. If the patient has active duodenal or gastric ulceration, thrombolysis might cause a haematemesis (vomiting of blood). Recent haemorrhagic strokes and recent operations will also be contraindications. A list of the major contraindications is shown in Table 2, but it must be emphasised that neither age nor severity of heart attack is a contraindication to treatment. The bigger the heart attack the more tissue there is to salvage. Diabetic retinopathy was a contraindication in

Active duodenal ulceration (within three months)
Recent cerebrovascular accident (stroke) (within six months)
Previous cerebral haemorrhage (ever)
Major surgery (within six weeks)
Known blood clotting abnormality
Uncontrolled hypertension (>200/110mmHg)

Table 2. The major contraindications to thrombolytic therapy.

the early 1990s, but no longer regarded as such.

Because streptokinase is a foreign tissue to the body, it stimulates the production of antibodies. This has two important effects relative to heart attacks. First, streptokinase may cause an immediate allergic reaction and give hypotension. Secondly, streptokinase induces antibodies which may remain in the body for years. A further dose of streptokinase at a later date will therefore be neutralised by these antibodies. Current practice is not to give streptokinase within six months of its first dose.

Once the patient is stable in casualty, he is transferred to the coronary care unit (or equivalent). The patient should reach the coronary care unit within 2–3 hours of the beginning of his myocardial infarction and will usually remain there for the next 48 hours. The function of the coronary care unit is the continuous monitoring of the patient's heart and other vital signs, the diagnosis and treatment of complications of a myocardial infarction, the confirmation of the diagnosis of a myocardial infarction and the institution of treatment to improve the overall prognosis of a myocardial infarction.

COMPLICATIONS OF A MYOCARDIAL INFARCTION

The early diagnosis and treatment of any complication is the reason for close monitoring once the patient reaches the coronary care unit. Table 3 shows some of the main complications which can occur after a myocardial infarction. In district general hospitals all these complications should be treatable apart from those which require angiography. Angiography is normally carried out in a tertiary referral centre or teaching hospital. Arrhythmias of one sort or

Cardiac arrest

Arrhythmias – tachycardias
brachycardias

Left (or right) ventricular failure

Cardiogenic shock

Ruptured mitral valve

Rupture interventricular septum

Rupture of the left ventricle

Pericarditis

Extension of infarction

Left ventricular aneurysm

Left ventricular thrombus and arterial embolus

Pulmonary embolus

Pericardial effusion and tamponade

Table 3. some of the main complications following a myocardial infarction.

another and heart failure are the most commonly occurring complications.

CONFIRMATION OF THE DIAGNOSIS OF MYOCARDIAL INFARCTION

The main investigations which distinguish myocardial pain from gastrointestinal or musculo-skeletal pain are serial ECGs and enzymes.

ECG

ECGs are done on a daily basis and occasionally more frequently. There may be no ECG changes at all in the first hour of a myocardial infarction, then the ST segment rises in the area of infarction due to injury. After a few hours Q-waves will develop indicating death of tissue, along with T-waves indicating ischaemic tissue. As the injured myocardium then becomes either ischaemic or dead, the ST segments will drop back to normal. Over a longer period of time the T-waves may become upright again, but if there has been death of tissue, Q-waves will remain permanently. There are many minor signs which might indicate myocardial insult of one sort or another, but it is the evolution of changes from admission which tend to confirm the presence or otherwise of a myocardial infarction.

Serum enzymes

Serum enzymes are substances released from dead and dying tissue which then circulate in the blood stream. There must a rise and fall of enzymes to

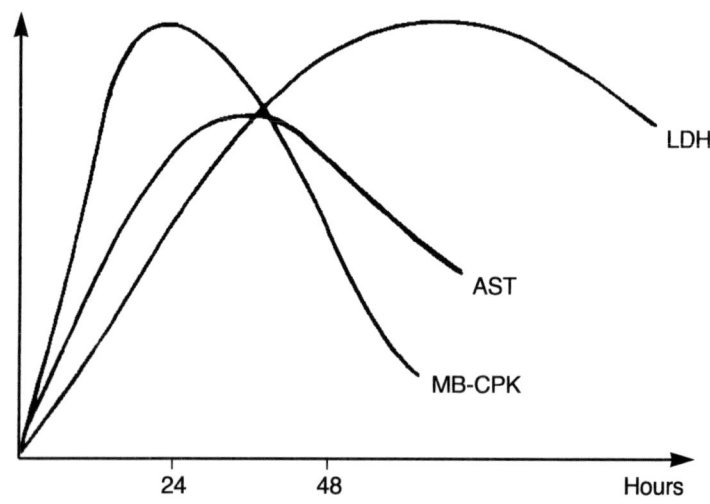

Figure 24. The release of serum enzymes after a myocardial infarction.

confirm a myocardial infarction (see Figure 24). The earliest enzyme to appear in the blood stream is creatinine phosphokinase (CPK), of which the MB fraction is relatively specific for heart muscle. Aspartate aminotransferase (AST) is the next enzyme likely to appear followed by lactic dehydrogenase (LDH). Care must be taken with the assessment of enzymes because, for example, liver damage can cause a rise in AST, skeletal damage a rise in CPK and pulmonary emboli a rise in LDH. Other insults to the body may increase enzymes to some degree, and some patients run a continually high enzyme level. It must be emphasised that the MBCPK enzyme is the only one which can give the diagnosis of a myocardial infarction with a high level of certainty.

TREATMENT TO IMPROVE PROGNOSIS

Aspirin

Aspirin in a dose of 75–300mg daily improves prognosis over the long term by up to 25%. Contraindications include peptic ulceration, but if possible all patients should be discharged on a daily dose.

Beta-blockers

In the absence of heart failure, beta-blockers have been shown to improve the mortality at the end of one year by 26% and the benefit is maintained for several years after. Because beta-blockers reduce the vigour of the heart, they are contraindicated in heart failure which often occurs with larger heart attacks. Beta-blockers have a number of side effects (see elsewhere) and Verapamil is a possible proven alternative.

ACE inhibitors

There is little doubt that ACE inhibitors improve the prognosis of patients with heart failure after a myocardial infarction by up to 25% at the end of one year. An increasing number of patients are being discharged on this drug.

Statins

A recent Scandinavian study (the 4S) showed a definite reduction in mortality and non-fatal myocardial infarctions by treating, with Simvastatin, those patients with raised total cholesterol.

Theoretically patients should be discharged from hospital, therefore, on aspirin, either beta-blockers or ACE inhibitors, and possibly a statin. This is not, however, an absolute rule and many contraindications to the use of these tablets may be present.

ON THE WARD

Most of the patients remain in the coronary care unit for about 48 hours and are then transferred to a medical ward for a further five days. Observation of the patient continues to a lesser degree and the patient is gradually mobilised. Most hospitals have a graduated exercise programme organised by a rehabilitation team. Cardiac rehabilitation improves life expectancy at three years by up to 20% after a myocardial infarction. It consists of exercises, education and psychological help. Reduction of risk factors is very important, eg stopping smoking, a low fat diet and weight loss. Cardiac rehabilitation will continue for several months after discharge.

FOLLOW-UP AFTER DISCHARGE

It is usual for patients to be followed up about six weeks after discharge, especially for an exercise test. The exercise test is extremely helpful in assessing prognosis after which patients will need further investigation. The DVLA recommends that patients resume driving (normal licence) at eight weeks post-infarction. However, at the discretion of the doctor this can occur as short as four weeks post-infarction. HGV licence holders have special regulations which will be dealt with in another chapter. The medical object at this time is to prevent a patient having further ischaemia or myocardial infarctions, and this may require him to have angiography followed by angioplasty and coronary artery bypass grafting.

PROGNOSIS

The principal factors which affect survival after a myocardial infarction are age and the size of the heart attack.

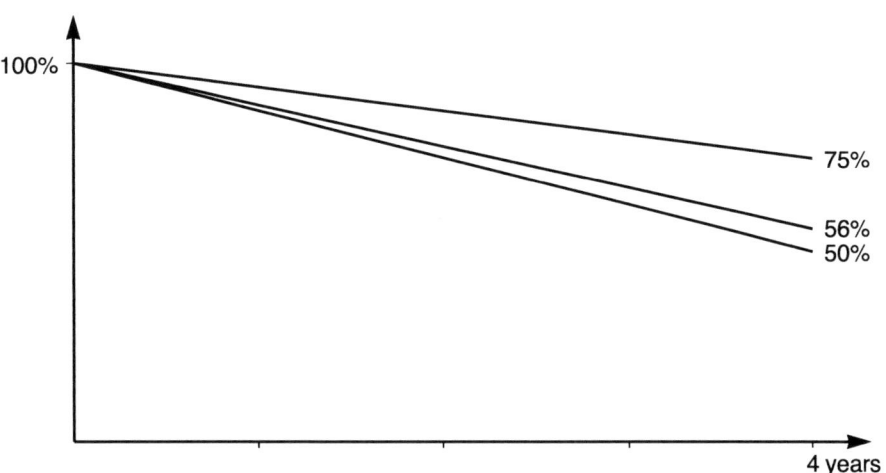

Figure 25. Four-year survival post-myocardial infarction with 1, 2, 3 vessel disease (narrowed as well).

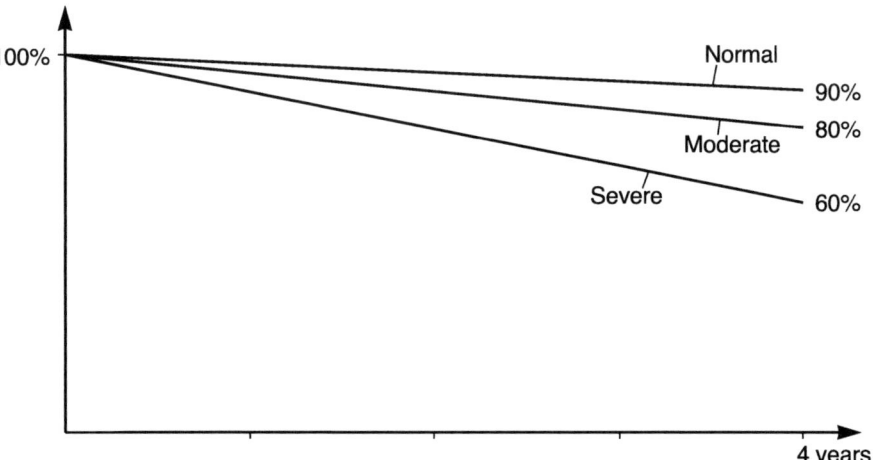

Figure 26. Four-year survival post-myocardial infarction according to degree of left ventricular dysfunction.

CHAPTER SEVEN

MEDICO-LEGAL ASPECTS OF CHEST PAIN, ANGINA AND MYOCARDIAL INFARCTION

STUDY OF CASES

In a recent personal study of 45 medico-legal cases from 1991 to 1995, 23 involved the problems of chest pain. The problem is almost invariably that the diagnosis of a myocardial infarction has been allegedly missed. Frequently these cases result in the death of the patient. Clearly this is an important medico-legal area and there are a number of reasons why such errors occur. It should be noted that there is often an overlap of causes.

Distinction from gastrointestinal pain

In a patient with a long history (years) of gastrointestinal symptoms it is always tempting to continue with the same diagnosis rather than consider that the pain might be myocardial. For example, the pain of a hiatus hernia or oesophageal spasm can be indistinguishable from that of a myocardial infarction. A patient is often only too willing to accept the diagnosis that his stomach or oesophagus is the cause of his pain and, unless the doctor is particularly vigilant, a wrong diagnosis may be made.

Importance of history-taking

In a third of the patients whose cases have resulted in medico-legal action involving chest pain, a history of angina is clearly written in the notes either by the GP or by the hospital doctors. In other words, the diagnosis had been missed despite the presence of the history being clearly available. It underlines the importance of being meticulous in taking a history and interpreting it.

Also, in a third of these cases there was a significant discrepancy between the history given by the patient and the history noted by the doctor. Many of the histories given by the patient's relatives clearly occur after the death of the patient. The discrepancy in the history is often dramatic and it may be difficult to be certain of what really happened. The only advice one can give here is that the doctor concerned must give as accurate a history in his notes as he possibly can.

Demands of relatives

The problem of abusive relatives occurred in a quarter of these patients. The difficulty is that a comparatively simple decision such as sending a patient into hospital becomes greatly aggravated when the relative concerned demands admission as a matter of emergency. This often sets up 'antibodies' in the doctor's mind, and he resists sending the patient in quickly because his judgement is being questioned. This can and indeed does lead to disaster. One must be careful to guard against this.

Failure to follow-up

Four of these cases arose as a result of failure of the patient to attend the out-patient department for follow-up visits. The problem here is who is responsible for remaking the appointment. The patient feels that if he does not come to an out-patient appointment then another one should be made for him if he really needs to attend. The hospital view tends to be that if a patient cannot be bothered to come, he must be perfectly well and there is no real point in making another appointment for him, particularly as out-patient clinics are so crowded. In the middle of this is the GP who presumably knows the patient well and who usually receives a note from the hospital saying that this patient has failed to come to out-patients and that he may or may not be sent a further appointment. Who is, therefore, responsible for these failed appointments?

With the very large out-patient clinics that take place in hospitals at the moment, especially in district general hospitals, there is an overwhelming feeling that it is the patient's responsibility to remake the appointment. The legal opinion at the present time (and this may, of course, change) is that it is both the hospital doctor and the GP's responsibility to make sure the patient attends his clinic appointment, especially for the follow-up of heart disease. The general principle is that the patient may not realise just how serious a condition he has and may not see a need to come back to out-patients when he feels reasonably well. This view could be disputed because, in the large clinics that occur in most hospitals these days, it is difficult to make sure that all patients return to the out-patients. It should perhaps be considered that the patient does have some responsibility for looking after himself.

Risk factors

It is clear from all the patients with chest pain in this particular group that the majority had significant risk factors, especially smoking. Therefore, if a doctor is faced with a patient with chest pains and the diagnosis is uncertain, he should pay particular attention to the patient who is smoking 40 cigarettes a day or who is a diabetic, etc. This sounds a simple comment, but in the cases concerned here it certainly was a factor.

Premature discharge of patients

Two of the patients in this particular group were discharged from hospital too quickly and sadly died a few hours later. Whilst it is easy to criticise this situation, it highlights the issue that most doctors in casualty departments are under great pressure not to admit patients. There are simply not enough beds. Medical Registrars would be embarrassed to admit a chest pain which turns out to be purely musculo-skeletal and bed managers ring up all junior doctors daily with a demand that they get their patients out immediately. It is a surprise to me that more medico-legal actions do not occur because of this particular problem, and it is clear from ordinary hospital practice that the number of complaints regarding early discharge has increased enormously in the last five years.

ECG interpretation

In a further two of these particular cases, the ECG performed in casualty was misread by the casualty officers. Unfortunately, both showed clear signs of ischaemia and, taken with chest pain, should have warranted admission of the patient. The question which arises is just how good a doctor should be at reading ECGs. Clearly a consultant should be better than casualty SHO, but the signs of ischaemia are taught from the first clinical year at medical school and these should be recognised by all doctors (T-wave changes, ST segment elevation and depression, Q-wave appearance).

GENERAL POINTS ABOUT CHEST PAINS, ETC

Clinical points

Timing of an MI

In medico-legal cases one is sometimes asked to state when a myocardial infarction actually occurred. It is not possible to be accurate in this situation, although extrapolating back from both ECG and enzyme changes one can get some indication of when the initial event probably occurred. The difficulty is that many patients have multiple pains, and it is often unclear which one actually started the myocardial infarction.

Prognosis

In terms of prognosis after the death of a patient from heart disease, the most important factor is how many coronary vessels were involved, how much narrowing was present in each of the arteries and what degree of damage there was to the left ventricle. Sadly this is often unclear from post-mortem reports, which can leave one hopelessly guessing at the prognosis.

Symptoms

The majority of cardiac patients feel perfectly well most of the time. This can be a trap for the unwary. Almost as soon as angina is relieved, a patient may feel completely normal.

Label of 'heart attack'

One must emphasise that the word 'heart attack' may sometimes be used inappropriately. A heart attack refers to a definite myocardial infarction with blockage of the coronary artery. To the public a heart attack might mean almost anything from a heart flutter to sudden death. Care must be taken before labelling a patient with a heart attack until absolutely certain.

Time delay in transfer

The time delay in obtaining a transfer from a district general hospital and teaching hospitals is increasingly problematic, eg for urgent angiography. It is very difficult to know when a delay becomes dangerous although it depends on each individual case. For example, a patient requiring angiography for unstable angina should be transferred to a teaching hospital within 2–3 days. If this wait becomes two weeks because of the lack of a bed and the patient should die, one wonders if the hospital or even the Government might be made responsible.

Routine medicals

Silent myocardial infarctions

Routine annual medicals are extremely common these days and many will turn up the possibility of a previous myocardial infarction unknown to the patient. This provides a dilemma. How much a doctor should tell a patient in such a situation when he is happily oblivious of the problem is an ethical one. Clearly the patient has a right to know exactly what is going on in his body, but if a patient is a born worrier, untold medical damage may be done by telling him he has had a heart attack and with it the thought that death is imminent. Clearly it is always an individual decision and certainly the patient's GP must be informed of the situation. He may be more aware if the patient could handle such a diagnosis. Some may have had indigestion and should, therefore, be followed up because the symptoms may represent current heart disease. Some 20% of all myocardial infarctions occur silently, especially if the patient is diabetic.

Failure of follow-up

The annual medical is specifically designed to prevent a problem occurring in the future. Therefore, if a patient presents with a history suggestive of angina, it must be carefully followed up. This did not happen in one particular medico-legal case and the patient died of a massive coronary three months later. It is very difficult to defend such an action, and those people performing annual medicals must be scrupulously careful to take note of the history, examination and results they have.

Licences

Where certain jobs require a very exacting medical, eg airline pilots, difficulties arise when a patient experiences chest pain. Because his job is on the line, he may be reluctant to admit his symptoms. If he does admit his chest pain, rigorous tests are necessary to obtain licences. These will be dealt with in a later chapter.

Cardiac medication

Nitrates in diagnosis

Patients are sometimes given a nitrate spray to see if it benefits them with regard to the chest pains. If it does, it does not automatically mean the chest pain is cardiac. A nitrate spray can relieve smooth muscle such as the oesophagus, although will usually take longer to do so. The giving of the nitrate spray, therefore, is not a diagnostic test of heart disease.

Thrombolysis

In the future there will undoubtedly be medico-legal cases involving thrombolysis. If a patient is given thrombolysis and suffers a haemorrhagic stroke, it is clear that the thrombolysis may have killed him. This is devastating to relatives, especially if the patient's chest pain is subsequently found to be non-cardiac. Unfortunately, even in the best hospitals this situation is always going to be a possibility. There is no test which can instantly diagnose a myocardial infarction and therefore action has to be taken on clinical grounds and early ECG evidence.

The risk of a haemorrhagic stroke is approximately 1% with tPA and 1.5% with streptokinase. When one considers that the mortality benefit is usually greater than 25%, it is reasonable to accept that the risk/benefit ratio is heavily weighted towards the benefit, ie it is justifiable to thrombolyse. Occasionally a similar situation will occur with a dissecting aortic aneurysm. Thrombolysis will exacerbate the bleeding into the inside layers of the aorta and undoubtedly hasten death. While some deaths may occur, the overall benefit of thrombolysis is enormous.

Ambulance

Ambulance response times to patients with chest pains have occasionally been criticised by relatives. Each of these has to be taken on its own merits, but all ambulance crews now log their times on a computer. When a relative is waiting for an ambulance to arrive, a couple of minutes usually feels like half an hour.

Aspirin

The giving of aspirin to a patient with chest pain at home is of considerable importance. It is a remarkably good thrombolytic agent and it should be automatic for all patients without contraindications to chew an aspirin as soon after the start of cardiac pain as possible. An article last year in the *British Medical Journal* indicated that this was only happening in about 60% of cases. In the future, failure to give aspirin in the early stages of a definite infarct may be considered negligent.

Beta-blockers

There are still occasions where patients receive inappropriate cardiac treatment: eg beta-blockers given to patients with asthma; thiazides given to patients and their potassium not checked; amiodarone given over a long period of time in too high a dose; and diamorphine given to patients with co-existent chest disease. All these problems are well known, but still do occur, and usually constitute negligence.

Drugs on discharge after myocardial infarction

Theoretically, patients being discharged following a myocardial infarction should be on aspirin, either a beta-blocker or an ACE inhibitor, and possibly a statin. Whilst there may be considerable contraindications to this particular practice, there is also a reluctance of physicians to put all patients routinely on these medications. Part of the reason is because all tablets have side effects, particularly beta-blockers, but as time goes by it may be difficult to defend doctors who have not put patients on the 'appropriate' treatment.

Tests for angina

Angiogram

Angiograms are invasive procedures and therefore have an inherent risk (see relevant chapter). Of the 45 cases described previously in this chapter, eight involved problems of angiography. In four of these cases there was inappropriate reading of the results of angiography; this is usually a matter for expert consideration. Four of the cases, however, involved damage to the brachial or femoral artery through which the catheter was introduced. Even in the best of hands this can occur, and it could not be described as negligent unless the procedure was done incorrectly or by an inexperienced operator. The risk is about 1.7% of such an episode happening, and must be considered as an acceptable risk. An embolus may rarely occur as a result of angiography causing a stroke for example, but unfortunately this is unavoidable even in the best of hands.

Racial difference of ECGs

There are racial differences in the shape of ECG tracings which can cause difficulty in diagnosing chest pains; eg raised ST segments are not uncommon in normal Afro-Caribbeans. This can give rise to confusion in such a patient who has chest pains. Unless there is a previous ECG available at that time showing the normal variation, the patient with chest pain may inevitably receive thrombolysis unnecessarily.

Athletic heart ECGs

A similar situation may occur in patients with athletic hearts. People who train vigorously often have bizarre looking ECGs, both raised ST segments and inverted T-waves. If a patient is young and athletic, it may be reasonable to assume the raised ST segment is related to this. However, a raised ST segment cannot be ignored in a patient with chest pain and this can lead to difficulties. Patients in their 40s who remain fit may be devastated by being told that they have an abnormality of their heart when they appear in casualty with musculo-skeletal chest pains. Great care must be taken in this situation including urgent cardiological referral.

Lost results

One of the problems that exists in medico-legal cases is lost reports. This is especially frustrating in a case of myocardial infarction where three consecutive days of ECGs and enzymes are required. Inevitably, in any system some results will become lost, and some enzymes may not be measured because the sample is 'lost'. Just how much responsibility the doctors and hospital have for providing accurate results on a daily basis is at the moment uncertain. Is the hospital negligent if a vital result goes missing?

CHAPTER EIGHT

CARDIAC ARREST

PROCEDURE

One of the most frightening events in a doctor's career is dealing with cardiac arrest. Generally speaking, resuscitation should occur in any patient who collapses unexpectedly from an unknown cause. When a patient is admitted, there should be some general indication whether such a procedure should be carried out in the event of the heart going into asystole or ventricular fibrillation. It may be that, if a patient is very ill with cancer, it is inappropriate to try and resuscitate them. Once a patient has been observed to have a cardiac arrest, the ABC of cardiac arrest comes into being.

A – Airway

B – Breathing

C – Cardiac massage

IMMEDIATE MANAGEMENT

The signs of a cardiac arrest are unconsciousness, the absence of spontaneous respiration, absent pulses and dilated pupils. The first person at a cardiac arrest should begin resuscitation and call for somebody to dial the cardiac arrest team. She should look for obstruction of the airway, remove pillows and clear the pharynx of food, vomit, foreign bodies and false teeth by gloved hand if possible (to prevent infection, especially Aids) and then deliver a sharp blow to the patient's chest. Occasionally this may suddenly restart the heart. Mouth to mouth resuscitation must be instituted either directly or using some form of airway through which breathing is possible. The neck must be extended during this time to open up the pharynx and larynx and the nose must be pinched to prevent air from escaping through the nasal passages.

Either the same person or the next person arising at the cardiac arrest should start cardiac massage. The heel of one hand should be placed over the lower third of the sternum and the other hand on top. The sternum should be compressed about 1.5–2in with an optimal pressure of 80–100lb. This weight is usually the weight of the upper half of the body of the resuscitator. The arm should be straight and the sternum should be compressed approximately 80 times per minute. Compression should occur quickly with a short pause for relaxation to allow blood to return to the heart. Artificial ventilation and cardiac massage should continue, together with a ratio of two inflations of the lungs to every 15 compressions of the heart. In this situation the patient may be kept resuscitatable for up to one hour.

ARRIVAL OF THE CARDIAC ARREST TEAM

Once the medical team has arrived a senior doctor must take charge to organise further resuscitative measures.

Ventilation

Mouth to mouth resuscitation is normally undertaken using an inflatable bag attached to an oxygen source of approximately 15 litres/min. Once the anaesthetist has arrived, endotracheal intubation should be performed so that the airway is absolutely clear.

Establishing an intravenous line

In order to get drugs rapidly into the heart to improve its function, an intravenous line must be inserted. A line is normally introduced through either an arm vein or in the neck. Through this line are infused specific cardiac drugs as well as bicarbonate to offset the acidosis which develops during cardiac arrest.

The ECG

An ECG monitor must be attached to the patient as soon as possible in order to establish the nature of the rhythm which has caused the cardiac arrest. This is usually asystole or ventricular fibrillation and rarely ventricular tachycardia.

ADVANCED CARDIAC RESUSCITATION

Defibrillation

If the patient has developed ventricular fibrillation, a shock applied to the chest of between 50–400 joules may restore sinus rhythm. This is delivered by a defibrillator and care must be taken not to shock bystanders who may be touching the body or bed.

Drugs

There is an enormous number of drugs which can be used to help the heart; for example, a very slow heart rate can be treated with Atropine and ventricular tachycardia can be treated with intravenous Lignocaine. Asystole may respond to adrenaline and isoprenaline and, once the heart starts to beat, numerous arrhythmias may occur which require an appropriate anti-arrhythmic drug.

Pacemaker

If the patient develops heart block following cardiac arrest, it is important to insert a temporary pacemaker to restore a normal rhythm.

THE CESSATION OF CARDIAC ARREST PROCEDURE

If the patient is fully resuscitated there is no difficulty in knowing when to curtail one's efforts. If, however, the procedure is clearly likely to be unsuccessful, someone has to take the decision to end the activity. This should be done with the senior doctor present who by then should know the full history of the patient and the problems which have occurred. The younger the patient, the longer one should continue resuscitation. It is possible to resuscitate people after an hour and half's cardiac arrest procedure provided that the underlying heart is not severely damaged in the first place. In the elderly patient half an hour of cardiac massage would certainly be long enough to indicate whether the heart will genuinely restart.

CONTROVERSY OF CARDIAC ARREST PROCEDURE

There is particular controversy as to whether a patient should be declared 'not for cardiac resuscitation', for whatever reason, when he is admitted to the ward and whether this instruction should remain throughout the patient's stay in hospital. A decision in this country is usually made by the medical staff taking note of all the circumstances of the patient. Clearly it is inappropriate to resuscitate a patient with a terminal illness only for him to die a painful death soon after. However, there are all shades of problems between that and the young, fit, healthy person who would be automatically resuscitated. There are still ongoing discussions as to whether relatives should be involved in this decision, and the medical ethics of this are complicated. One should remember that asking a close relative to agree to a patient not being resuscitated may result in guilt feelings later in life.

CHAPTER NINE

HEART FAILURE

INTRODUCTION

There is no adequate definition of heart failure except that it is a situation in which the heart is not providing the organs with sufficient blood. This is, in effect, a reduced cardiac output. The problems caused by failure of the heart to pump blood adequately into the body results in forward failure, ie inadequate cardiac output, and backward failure, ie back pressure into the lungs. These phases have been in existence since James Hope described them in 1832, but have been more recently rediscovered as systolic (forward) and diastolic (backward) failure.

CAUSES OF HEART FAILURE

Heart failure may be divided into volume overload, pressure overload, poor myocardial function, arrhythmias, and as a result of influences from outside the heart.

Volume overload

An example of this is aortic regurgitation. Every time the heart pumps, a larger quantity of blood must be ejected because a certain amount regurgitates into the heart. A greater volume, therefore, is transmitted with every contraction and this is referred to as volume overload. Continuous volume overload eventually results in failure as the muscle becomes exhausted. Other examples of this would be mitral regurgitation, shunts and, rarely, vitamin B_1 deficiency.

Pressure overload

Pressure overload occurs when the left ventricle develops a greater systolic pressure to expel its contents than normal. This occurs eg when high blood pressure is left untreated and the ventricle becomes hypertrophied. Subsequently, the failing muscle will become weak and tired due to the continuous, high pressure. Other examples of pressure overload are aortic stenosis and co-arctation of the aorta.

Myocardial failure

Any process which damages the left ventricular muscle will cause heart failure. The commonest example of this is coronary artery disease where a myocardial infarction may cause the heart to fail. Cardiomyopathies are another example of which there are numerous causes.

Arrhythmias

Any very fast or very slow heart rhythm will result in heart failure. For example, the sudden onset of atrial fibrillation with a heart rate of approximately 180/min is frequently associated with the development of cardiac failure.

Outside influences upon the heart

Excessive hormone production such as hyperthyroidism, a phaeochromo-cytoma and Cushing's syndrome will all cause the heart to alter its function and later to fail.

TREATMENT OF CARDIAC FAILURE

The cause of the heart failure should be treated if at all possible. If, for example, heart failure is caused by aortic regurgitation, aortic valve replacement would be appropriate. If high blood pressure is the cause of cardiac failure, it must be reduced with medication. However, in the majority of patients heart failure is myocardial in origin and medication is necessary, ie diuretics and ACE inhibitors.

Diuretics

One of the initial compensatory mechanisms which occur in heart failure is the retention of sodium and water. This increases the pre-load on the heart, making it work harder and increasing the cardiac output. Unfortunately, when this mechanism over-compensates and excessive sodium and water are retained, overloading of the heart occurs and fluid accumulates both in the lungs and the body in general. When it accumulates in the lung area it causes breathlessness. When water accumulates generally it descends by gravity to the lowest part of the body, ie ankles, but if lying in bed, the sacral area. To remove this unwanted water, diuretics are used either intravenously or orally. Where a patient suddenly goes into heart failure with copious amounts of fluid in the lungs, an intravenous diuretic can solve the problem in a matter of

30–60 minutes. Patients can be maintained on a daily dose of diuretics taken orally for many years.

ACE inhibitors

By dilating the blood vessels in the body, the heart will pump against a reduced after-load. This allows a greater stroke volume and increased cardiac output. The most effective tablets for this are called angiotensin-converting enzyme (ACE) inhibitors. Angiotensin is the most powerful vasoconstrictor known within the body. It is produced in excess in heart failure and, by inhibiting the process by which the active metabolite is created, the vasoconstriction becomes vasodilatation. ACE inhibitors are highly effective, resulting in increased quantity and quality of life. Taking all ACE inhibitor trials together, there was about a 25% improvement in life expectancy after one or more years of daily therapy.

Digoxin

Digoxin has been used for heart failure since William Withering discovered its use in 1785, and is still the only drug which improves contractility of the left ventricle without exhausting it. Its value is relatively mild compared with ACE inhibitors and diuretics, but it is still particularly useful if the patient has a persistently fast heart rate at rest.

OTHER TREATMENT OF HEART FAILURE

Surgical approaches for treatment of heart failure can be beneficial in certain circumstances, eg a valve replacement for valvular heart disease. However, despite it seeming logical, coronary artery bypass grafting has no benefit whatever on cardiac failure. If the heart muscle is badly damaged and drug treatment begins to fail completely, a cardiac transplantation can be considered. This is usually reserved for patients under the age of 55 because of the lack of donor hearts. This is an excellent procedure with a three year life expectancy of at least 80%, and the problems of rejection have now largely been overcome by the advent of cyclosporin.

Another possible surgical procedure to help heart failure is the conversion of ordinary muscle, eg the pectoral muscles (the front of the chest) or the latissimus dorsi (the back muscles of the chest), into cardiac muscle. The pectoral muscles can be mobilised with an intact nervous and arterial supply and attached in the area where the heart is damaged. With the use of a pacemaker and repetitive stimulation, the skeletal muscle can actually become heart muscle. This whole procedure is still in its relatively early stages, but promises to be valuable in the future.

CHAPTER TEN

HYPERTENSION

INTRODUCTION

Hypertension is a relatively new disease which was discovered when accurate methods of measuring blood pressure were developed in the 1920s. It is extremely unfortunate that the name given to high blood pressure was 'hypertension'. It is meant to indicate that the tension of the arteries has increased and so causes a rise in the blood pressure. Unfortunately the population at large believes that it means hypertension is caused by stress. There is no evidence for this whatsoever.

The second major problem with hypertension is that many doctors find it unrewarding. This is because, in the majority of cases, most patients do not have any symptoms whatsoever, but once on medication begin to suffer from the side effects of the pills.

Hypertension is remarkably common and may affect 9–15% of the adult population, ie probably more than six million people in this country. It is consequently of great importance and, because it may damage the heart, brain and kidney if left unchecked, it must be sought out and looked after with care. The majority of a GP's patients will visit him over a five year period, and this is why most patients will have their blood pressure taken when they attend for some other illness. An average GP practice consisting of 7,500 patients has 500 patients with mildly-high blood pressure, 50 with moderately-high blood pressure and five with severely-high blood pressure.

THE INTERPRETATION OF THE BLOOD PRESSURE

There are two readings of blood pressure, the highest recorded in the artery (systolic) and the lowest pressure reached in the artery (diastolic). A rise above normal of either or both of these figures may result in problems. Blood pressure within the population is a continuous variable. There are not two distinct populations, one with normal blood pressure and one with high blood pressure. Therefore, the cut-off point where blood pressure must be considered high and therefore treatable has been hotly debated for generations. The upper limit of normal on the WHO criteria is 140/95, but as a result of many trials the majority of doctors take 160/100 as being the upper limit of normal.

It is true that the lower the blood pressure, the less likely you are to have complications of high blood pressure. This, however, is different from saying that, if you reduce the diastolic blood pressure with medication from say 90 to 80, the patient will benefit. A few years ago three major trials, one British, one Australian and one American, looked at what was then described as mild, ie diastolic, blood pressure from 90–105mmHg. The benefits within this group were not great, and it is from these studies that the cut-off figure of 100 is largely regarded as the starting point of high blood pressure.

Diastolic blood pressure of 90–100 is regarded as borderline, 100–105 mild, 105–120 moderate, and greater than 120 severe. There is a relatively rare form of high blood pressure which is called accelerated or malignant, when a very high blood pressure suddenly develops in a patient whose previous pressure has been relatively normal. This carries particular dangers, with the diastolic pressure often being 140 or more.

The upper limit of systolic blood pressure is even more difficult to define. It used to be said that the upper limit of normal was approximately 100 plus one's age. This is not really true. There is a gradual rise of blood pressure with age, but at the age of 70, the blood pressure of 160 systolic would still be regarded as the upper limit of normal. Systolic hypertension is commoner in the elderly patient when age stiffens the arteries, and in recent trials this has been shown to be an important risk factor.

THE DANGER OF HIGH BLOOD PRESSURE

High blood pressure damages the arteries. It may do so by causing an increased thickening of the arterial wall. As the wall thickens, the lumen of the arteries becomes smaller and reduces the flow. High blood pressure also encourages the development of atheroma which causes further narrowing of a probably already narrowed lumen. Finally, micro-aneurysms (tiny balloon-like protrusions from the wall of the artery) may develop and subsequently rupture causing bleeding into the organ concerned. The brain, the heart and the kidneys are the organs most susceptible to problems of high blood pressure, producing strokes, heart attacks and kidney failure.

THE TAKING OF BLOOD PRESSURE

There is little doubt that this is one of the more difficult aspects of medicine as a whole. Blood pressure is never the same two minutes running and may vary in the ordinary patient from 140 systolic in the afternoon to 80 systolic in the middle of the night. Therefore, the taking of a casual reading when the patient goes to the GP is fraught with difficulty. Blood pressure is never diagnosed on a single recording and the minimum numbers of casual readings taken before blood pressure can be diagnosed is three. Some patients, however, put their blood pressures up rapidly at the sight of a doctor, even though they may have known him for 20 years. This may be related to fear or a more deep seated reflex, and clearly causes diagnostic difficulties.

If a patient's blood pressure is only up at the sight of the doctor, blood pressure, at times, may be reduced by treatment to below normal. This would make the patient feel ill and could be dangerous in the elderly. Therefore, multiple recordings must be taken in a variety of ways. Firstly, there is the 24 hour blood pressure monitoring device which records the blood pressure, say, every half an hour through the whole 24 hours. Secondly, there is an automatic blood pressure machine for the patient to take his own blood pressure at home.

There is still debate as to which is the most accurate measure of the blood pressure, but all the major trials have been done on casual recordings of blood pressure at the doctor's surgery. The taking of blood pressure is influenced by circumstances, eg a full bladder, cold weather or pain. These all slightly increase the blood pressure. It is also important to have the right size of cuff when taking a blood pressure, especially if a patient has a very large arm.

SYMPTOMS OF BLOOD PRESSURE

The idea that blood pressure always causes headaches and nose bleeds is completely erroneous. It is true that some patients with high blood pressure complain of headaches and muzziness, but this is very much the exception rather than the rule. Nose bleeds are usually due to rupture of veins and have nothing to do with high blood pressure at all. Once an organ has been damaged by blood pressure, symptoms may occur from that. For example, if the heart has been badly dilated by high blood pressure and begins to fail, the patient may present with severe breathlessness. The vast majority of patients who are diagnosed with high blood pressure have no symptoms whatsoever.

THE SIGNS OF HIGH BLOOD PRESSURE

Usually there are no signs at all of high blood pressure other than the reading. Occasionally there are signs at the back of the eye and enlargement of the heart or renal abnormalities which can be detected, but by and large most patients will be absolutely normal. Occasionally there will be a secondary cause for blood pressure and the symptoms and signs will be those of the primary cause, eg Cushing's syndrome can present with high blood pressure, but it would be obvious from the physical signs, ie the round moon face, etc., that Cushing's syndrome was the problem and high blood pressure was purely a secondary issue.

THE CRITERIA FOR TREATMENT

The current situation is that borderline blood pressure is watched carefully and treatment is only instituted once the diastolic blood pressure reaches 100 or more on a regular basis, although this might be slightly different in the elderly patient. A middle-aged patient with a blood pressure of 160/100 will live approximately 14 years less than an equivalent patient with a blood pressure of 120/80. The greater the pressure left untreated, the greater the risk. Moderately high blood pressure (diastolic 105–120) carries a 20% mortality at the end of five years if left untreated, and severe hypertension carries a 60% mortality over the same period of time if left untreated. If the blood pressure is borderline, but there is evidence of damage to the brain, heart or kidneys, reducing the blood pressure is beneficial. Evidence of loss of function in the brain, heart or kidneys is known as end organ damage, and it is for evidence of this that the patient is investigated.

THE CAUSES OF HIGH BLOOD PRESSURE

In about 99.5% of patients who have high blood pressure no treatable cause can be found. In approximately 80% of patients there is no abnormality within the body whatsoever, and in approximately 19.5% there will be some evidence of renal damage. There is nothing that can be done about kidney damage in this situation apart from correct the blood pressure. Only in the very tiny minority is there a cause for blood pressure which can be treated, and this is called secondary hypertension. There are four important causes:

(a) endocrine, eg Cushing's syndrome or Conn's syndrome;

(b) hormonal, eg the contraceptive pill;

(c) co-arctation of the aorta; and

(d) drugs such as steroids and non-steroidal anti-inflammatory agents, eg Voltarol.

INVESTIGATION OF THE PATIENT

Because the secondary causes of high blood pressure are so rare, one has to be sensible about how far to investigate a patient with high blood pressure. It is inappropriate to do costly tests looking for the rare Cushing's syndrome on every patient who presents with high blood pressure. Therefore, the routine investigations on a patient should include:

(a) ophthalmoscopy for evidence of hypertensive retinopathy – this is looking at the blood vessels at the back of the eye to see if they have become thickened and tortuous. In extreme cases there will be swelling of the optic disc as well (known as papilloedema);

(b) blood for potassium (a low result will indicate Conn's syndrome), creatinine (a high reading will indicate renal damage), glucose (if diabetes is also present, it represents a significant heart risk) and a haemoglobin (a low level might indicate chronic renal failure);

(c) measuring the protein in the urine – in any significant quantity this may well represent evidence of renal damage;

(d) a chest X-ray – normally performed when looking for evidence of an enlarged heart, although this is a very rare occurrence in routine blood pressure patients. It will also pick up evidence of co-arctation of the aorta; and

(e) an ECG – this may indicate enlargement or strain of the left ventricle, indicative of end organ damage from blood pressure.

FURTHER INVESTIGATION

Patients who should be further investigated fall into three groups:

(a) younger patients, eg those under 45 years;

(b) those with resistant blood pressure, ie which refuses to come under control with normal medication; and

(c) those with rapidly rising blood pressure – this is blood pressure which has been mild but becomes severe.

These patients have a higher proportion of secondary causes of hypertension. In these patients effort should be made to see if there is any evidence of Cushing's syndrome, a phaeochromocytoma, Conn's syndrome, renal artery stenosis, co-arctation of the aorta or inappropriate drug history.

THE TREATMENT OF BLOOD PRESSURE

Medication is not the only treatment for high blood pressure. Some reduction can be achieved by the patient modifying his lifestyle, although this is rarely likely to eliminate the problem altogether.

Non-pharmacological

Salt

It is a contentious issue as to whether reducing salt intake will actually reduce high blood pressure. Small reductions may be possible from a moderate salt reduction, but the diet of severe salt reduction is so unpalatable that few would be prepared to try. Reduction in blood pressure would seldom be more than 5%.

Obesity

There is little doubt that obesity is related to blood pressure. Reduction in weight will reduce blood pressure and may change a borderline blood pressure into a normal one.

Alcohol

Drinking more than six units of alcohol per day will increase the blood pressure in susceptible patients; if such patients stop drinking alcohol, their blood pressures will return to their pre-alcohol levels. In other words, the patient with high blood pressure who is drinking more than a quarter of a bottle of Scotch a day would certainly benefit greatly from stopping drinking.

Exercise

Moderate exercise may be mildly beneficial for those with high blood pressure. It is usually associated with a fall in weight and hence it is difficult to know whether it is the exercise or the weight reduction which is relevant. Fortunately, mild/moderate exercise seems to be as good as vigorous exercise.

Stress

Acute stress causes a sudden rise in blood pressure, but whether background stress causes a continuous rise in blood pressure is not known. If a person is maliciously attacked with a knife their blood pressure will rise. This does not mean they have high blood pressure. Whilst great emphasis used to be placed on relief of stress, this is not now a factor that attracts much concern.

Cigarette smoking

Cigarette smoking is a powerful risk factor in its own right and, with high blood pressure, causes marked increase in risk. Consequently, any hypertensive patient who smokes must be strongly urged to quit. Cigarette smoking itself has little direct effect upon blood pressure in the long term.

Pharmacological

It is always possible to reduce someone's blood pressure. All one needs to do is remove six pints of blood and the blood pressure will drop to very low level. The problem is, therefore, one of side effects. This is particularly relevant with drugs, as most drugs will reduce the blood pressure to a varying degree. The problem that arises is with the adverse effects they cause.

There is no particular order in which drugs should be used and every doctor will have his own favourite regime. In general, the recommendation is to start with thiazide diuretics and/or beta-blockers and then to move on to other antihypertensive agents. However, beta-blockers and thiazide diuretics probably have more side effects than other tablets, which is why we have seen a rise in the use of tablets like ACE inhibitors as first-use drugs in the last five years.

Thiazide diuretics

These tablets work partly by diuresis and also by reducing sodium content. The side effects include postural hypotension, high blood sugar, low blood potassium, high uric acid, slightly high cholesterol and, perhaps most important of all, impotence. These effects are dose related, but one must take care even with small doses. Perhaps the most important aspect of diuretics is that the potassium should be taken approximately one month after starting the tablets to ascertain if the patient is losing too much potassium. If there is no significant loss of potassium in the early stages, it is unlikely it will occur later. This is important because low potassium can lead to arrhythmias.

Beta-blockers

Beta-blockers are widely used for blood pressure as well as angina. The main problem is the side effects of weariness and dreariness which occur with almost every beta-blocker. In addition there are problems of leaden legs when walking, bronchospasm in the susceptible, precipitating potential heart failure, and peripheral vasoconstriction which leads to cold hands and feet. Although there are different types of beta-blockers, some of which have fewer side effects, all can precipitate severe asthma in a susceptible subject.

Calcium antagonists

Calcium antagonists dilate the peripheral blood vessels. Such dilatation of blood vessels causes headache, facial flushing and ankle oedema along, at times, with postural hypotension.

ACE inhibitors

ACE inhibitors also dilate blood vessels but in a different manner to calcium antagonists. They have fewer side effects, although approximately 20% of patients will have a dry, irritating cough. Combined with large doses of diuretic, they can produce an initial, dramatic drop in blood pressure which should be avoided. Newer drugs, ACE blockers, give many of the benefits of ACE inhibitors without the dry cough.

Other hypotensive agents

The newer alpha-blockers like Doxasozin also dilate blood vessels and can be useful, although their side effects can be similar to the calcium antagonists. Methyldopa has been used for a great many years for high blood pressure and works by reducing the amount of adrenaline in the body in general. Whilst it can be effective, it can cause sleepiness as well as impotence and postural hypotension.

THE FOLLOW-UP OF PATIENTS WITH HIGH BLOOD PRESSURE

Once a patient has been diagnosed as having either suspected or definite high blood pressure, follow-up is fairly frequent until it is under control. Thereafter the blood pressure is usually taken about once every three months and, depending on the tablets used, the patient should probably have a blood test once a year for potassium and creatinine.

RAISED BLOOD PRESSURE IN SPECIFIC GROUPS OF PATIENTS

Blood pressure in pregnancy

This is a very specialised area. Patients may start pregnancy with high blood pressure, may develop blood pressure during pregnancy or may develop pre-eclamptic toxaemia, a sign of which is high blood pressure. The management of this is usually by an obstetrician, but it is important to note that some antihypertensive agents can damage the foetus. The drugs which have been proven to be safe in pregnancy are the beta-blockers – Atenolol, Propranolol and Labetalol (this is a combined beta and alpha-blocker) – and methyldopa. ACE inhibitors, for example, can be tetrogenic.

The elderly

There has been debate whether it is reasonable to continue treating patients for high blood pressure as they get older, especially with the increasing incidence of side effects from tablets. However, several major trials have demonstrated the value of antihypertensive agents, particularly when the systolic blood pressure is high. Therefore, it is important to treat this group, especially if there has been previous evidence of end organ damage.

Children

It was postulated that, by taking children's blood pressure once a year, it would be possible to track those patients who would eventually develop blood pressure later in life and, by salt restriction, etc, reduce this likelihood. However, tracking of children in this way in the US has not proven to be of any value at all. It is rare, therefore, to take children's blood pressure regularly, but it is important to take it if a child presents with symptoms such as headache.

Racial differences

West Indians have a particularly resistant type of blood pressure; eg they do not respond well to beta-blockers.

Resistant blood pressure

This is blood pressure which fails to be controlled despite all the normal pharmacological measures. Whilst this may be related to poor prescribing by the physician and poor patient co-operation (ie not taking tablets), there is undoubtedly a group in which the blood pressure refuses to come down despite every effort. These cases need investigating for evidence of secondary high blood pressure, especially renal artery stenosis, but it is always worth checking whether these patients are actually taking their drugs, or are drinking an excess of alcohol.

MEDICO-LEGAL ASPECTS OF HIGH BLOOD PRESSURE

Failure of follow-up

Fortunately, blood pressure rarely features in medico-legal actions. This is because it is a long, drawn-out illness and it is seldom possible to identify a specific action that may have been inappropriate. Perhaps the commonest problem is the failure of follow-up in a patient with known high blood pressure. Once controlled, blood pressure should be followed up approximately every three months, but not infrequently a patient forgets to return for a check. Most practices will not prescribe drugs after three months until the patient has been seen. This is a reasonably foolproof method.

Pre-eclampsia

Pre-eclampsia and high blood pressure in pregnancy is a particularly difficult area of management, and concerns obstetrics rather than a book on cardiovascular disease.

Children

The occasional medico-legal case has arisen because blood pressure has not been taken in children who have been suffering from headaches or blurred vision. This is rare, but one must always be on guard for this.

Secondary causes

Occasionally a secondary cause of high blood pressure is missed for some time. Because of the rarity of secondary causes and the large number of high blood pressure cases, it would be impossible to do all the tests for secondary hypertension on every patient. However, care must be taken in patients who are young, those with resistant high blood pressure or those with rapidly rising blood pressure. In particular these patients should be checked for renal artery stenosis. Females tend to develop this at a young age due to causes unknown, and men usually at an older age when atheroma causes the narrowing.

Beta-blockers

Occasionally, as with angina, beta-blockers are given to patients who suffer from an asthmatic tendency. This can, of course, be disastrous and must at all costs be avoided. No beta-blocker is safe in this situation.

Lack of treatment

A thought provoking suggestion first made in the 1960s is that half the patients with high blood pressure in this country have not been diagnosed, half the remaining patients are not treated at all and, finally, half of those who have been treated were not being adequately treated. In other words, only one eighth of the patients have been correctly treated for high blood pressure. If this is true, it leaves a vast population of patients waiting to sue their doctors.

In the UK 'the deaths from preventable, hypertension-related disease are equivalent to one fully laden jumbo jet crashing and killing all passengers every six weeks'. I think it is unlikely that the present situation is as bad as this, but it gives some indication of the seriousness with which we should view hypertension.

Lack of symptoms

There is a case of a patient (a docker) who presented asymptomatically with the co-incidental problem of high blood pressure. The systolic blood pressure was off the top of the scale on the mercury manometer (greater than 300mmHg) and the diastolic was 160mmHg. Because the patient did not feel he had any symptoms from his high blood pressure, he totally refused treatment. He was dead within a year. This underlines the problem that some patients, even those with very high blood pressure, can be completely asymptomatic, as well as the need for proper compliance in taking the tablets.

CHAPTER ELEVEN

ARRHYTHMIAS

INTRODUCTION

The feeling of the pulse and its various irregularities was observed by the Chinese as far back as 2700 BC. In 1707, a famous book written by Sir John Floyer – *The Physicians Pulse Watch* – noted over 300 pages of different diagnoses that could be made directly on feeling the pulse, most of which originated from the Chinese. But the exact nature of arrhythmias was not known until Sir James MacKenzie recorded irregular rhythms on his polygraph. This was a pen and ink method of recording directly from the pulse showing its variations.

However, it was left predominantly to Sir Thomas Lewis as a result of his work on the ECG to write a book in the 1920s which included almost every arrhythmia that we know today. The ECG is still the best way of diagnosing an arrhythmia, although electro-physiological studies which record the electricity from within the heart may provide more accurate knowledge.

An arrhythmia is any abnormal rhythm of the heart, and can produce a variety of symptoms including palpitations, light headedness, dizziness, funny turns and syncope. The word palpitation simply means an awareness of the heart beating and does not imply a particular type of arrhythmia. The majority of people will have had some form of arrhythmia during their lifetime. Most will have some form of extra beats known as ectopic beats, with atrial fibrillation being the next most frequent arrhythmia. Almost all patients who have palpitations will be frightened by them because the heart is involved, but palpitations are seldom dangerous.

An abnormal heart rhythm only becomes a significant problem if there is evidence of underlying heart disease. In the majority of young people where hearts are normal all manner of arrhythmias may occur without endangering life at all. In the elderly person it is more likely that heart disease is the cause of the arrhythmia and therefore potential problems can occur. Arrhythmias occurring in the presence of heart disease cause problems either because they are inherently dangerous and may lead to cardiac arrest or because they produce heart failure. Problems of palpitations and arrhythmias count for up to a quarter of cardiological out-patient visits to any district general hospital.

Arrhythmias can be divided into three groups: ectopic beats, tachycardias and bradycardias.

ECTOPICS

Definition

An ectopic beat is one which originates from a different place to the normal origin of the heart beat, the sinus node. It is a single beat and may arise from the atrial area, the area around the AV node (the junctional area) or the ventricular area (see Figure 27).

The nature of the ectopic beat

After each normal beat of the heart there is a inhibitory period which prevents any other electrical activity of the heart. The sinus node beats regularly and the ectopic beat can only fire between the end of the electrically inhibitory period and the next beat. Therefore, it will always arise earlier than expected, and its own electrical inhibitory period will prevent the next firing of the sinus node. The sinus node will fire but will be blocked and will have to restart at its normal cycle length and come in again after the ectopic beat.

This leaves a gap between the ectopic beat and the next beat which is longer than expected and is known as the compensatory pause. It is this

Figure 27. Atrial ectopic beats.

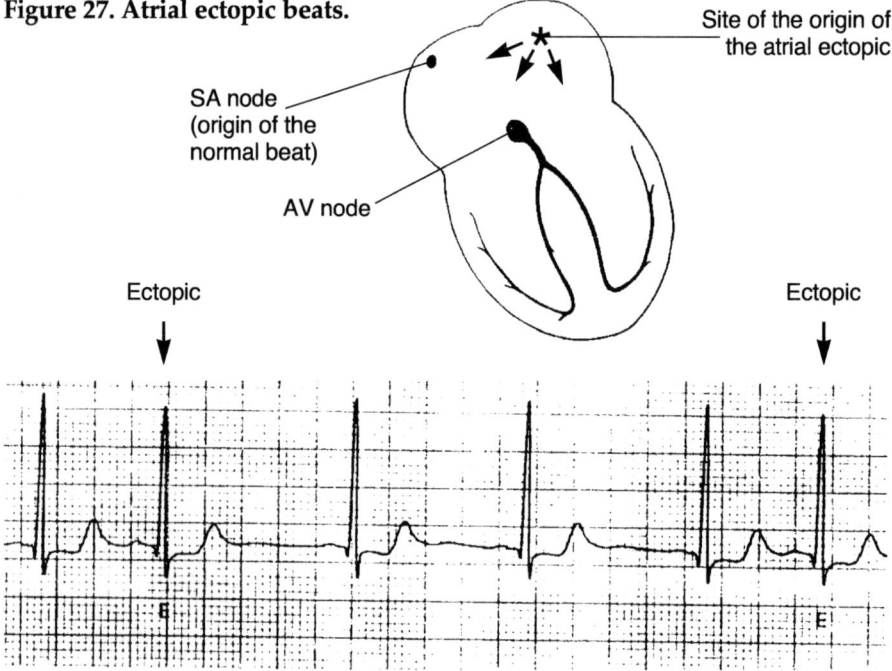

irregularity which causes all the problems. The gap between the initial sinus beat and the ectopic beat is very short and therefore, when contraction occurs, the pulse is very small. However, the normal beat, after the ectopic beat, occurs after a long filling period. This means that the next normal beat is much stronger and may feel like a thud in the chest. All types of ectopic beats have this particular sequence. Occasionally extra beats or 'ectopic' beats can occur when the sinus node fails to beat for any reason, but these are usually called escape beats rather than ectopic beats.

Symptoms

A sudden thud in the chest due to the beat after the ectopic beat is a common symptom, and patients may well notice the pause when they think their heart is not going to start again. This tends to produce a very anxious feeling in the chest and the sudden thud or gap will produce an anxiety feeling that may take the breath away. The rush of the blood from post-ectopic beat often gives a curious tickling sensation in the neck and throat.

Signs

The pulse will feel regularly irregular or irregularly irregular. This will become more apparent when various arrhythmias are discussed.

Significance of ectopic beats

By far the majority of ectopic beats are completely innocent unless there is known heart disease. They are also extremely common. All types of ectopic beats – atrial, junctional or ventricular – will occur almost as frequently as one's age; in other words 30% of 30 year olds will have occasional ectopic beats, as will 50% of 50 year olds, and this will rise to 100% of 70 year olds. Such ectopics would be picked up on a routine 24 hour tape and many patients will not realise they are having them. Even with ischaemic heart disease or cardiomyopathy, ectopic beats are not necessarily signs of danger. In certain valve abnormalities, eg mitral valve prolapse, ectopic beats are present in almost everyone, but again are completely benign.

Ectopic beats become significant immediately after a myocardial infarction. Within the first 24–48 hours ectopic beats can sometimes lead to serious arrhythmias and therefore need treatment with intravenous Lignocaine. However, even these ectopics are less seriously considered than perhaps 10 or 15 years ago.

Treatment of ectopic beats

Where the ectopic beats are not associated with heart disease there is usually no necessity for medical treatment. There is no increased mortality from ectopic beats and the beats will not 'wear out' the heart. With strong reassurance, the patient may well find the sensation of ectopic beats will disappear. Once the brain has got used to the concept of ectopic beats it will tend to ignore them rather like when one wears a hat; one is conscious of the presence of it for the first few minutes and then forgets about it altogether.

Because the biggest problem with ectopic beats is the anxiety and worry that they cause, beta-blockers are probably the first line of treatment. This will effectively dampen the feeling of the ectopic. Anxiety potentiates the post-ectopic beat which makes it more uncomfortable. Occasionally this can be so bad that the patient is frightened and collapses in fear. If the patient is an asthmatic or cannot tolerate beta-blockers, other anti-arrhythmic agents can be used, eg Verapamil, Amiodarone or Diltiazem.

TACHYCARDIAS

A tachycardia is present when the heart rate is more than 100 beats per minute.

The origin of tachycardias

Figure 28 shows two types of tachycardia, one regular and the others slightly irregular. Although it is not known precisely how the electro-physiological abnormality which produces tachycardias occurs, it is thought to be due to a circuit motion around two pathways from one part of the heart to the other. As long as both paths conduct equally there is no problem with conduction of the electrical signal from top to bottom of the heart, but if one pathway is temporarily blocked a continuous circuit motion is produced, resulting in re-entry tachycardia (Figure 28).

Symptoms

A rapid heart rate usually results in the fall of blood pressure, creating light headedness. dizziness, funny turns and occasionally syncope. Where there is underlying heart disease there may well be further symptoms related to this, eg angina or breathlessness. The majority of tachycardias will start abruptly (like a switch turning on) and stop equally suddenly. This distinguishes it from a sinus tachycardia caused by adrenaline release where the onset will be relatively slow and disappearance equally so. Most tachycardias will be described as rapid and tapping, whilst tachycardias caused by adrenaline release will be heavy, thudding and not as rapid.

**Figure 28. The mechanism
of re-entry tachycardias.**

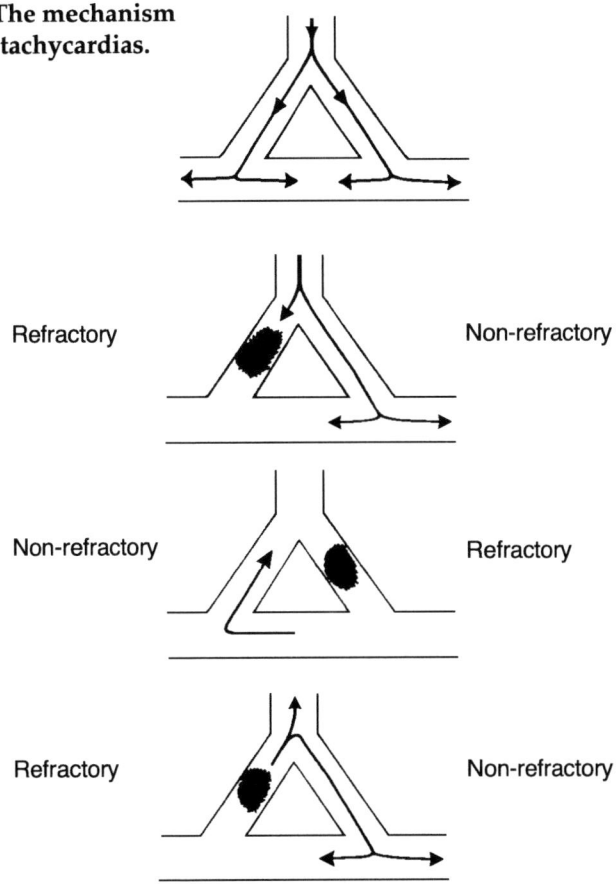

Refractory   Non-refractory

Non-refractory   Refractory

Refractory   Non-refractory

Signs

The pulse will normally demonstrate the tachycardia readily, but when the heart rate reaches more than about 150 it may not be possible to palpate the tachycardia at the wrist. It may be necessary to listen to the heart directly in order to hear the actual rate of the tachycardia.

Investigations

The ordinary ECG rarely catches a tachycardia which is frequently intermittent and transient. A 24 hour ECG tape recording is performed, although clearly this may not always record the offending arrhythmia. Sometimes a 24 hour tape must be repeated several times or substituted with a longer tape, eg 48 hours.

Types of tachycardia

Supraventricular tachycardias

These are tachycardias which originate from above the ventricle and conduct in a normal way through the bundle of His to the ventricular muscle. An irregular tachycardia would be found in atrial fibrillation or atrial tachycardia with varying block, whereas a regular tachycardia would be found in atrial flutter and a normal supraventricular tachycardia.

Ventricular tachycardias

For ease of description ventricular tachycardias are often described as narrow or broad complex according to the length of time of the QRS configuration. The definitions are not particularly clinically orientated, but enable a more accurate diagnosis.

Treatment

Because tachycardias are more likely to result in heart failure, especially in a patient with underlying heart disease, it may be necessary to restore normal rhythm as a matter of urgency. This can be achieved by DC cardioversion, ie passing an electric shock through the chest. This is performed under general anaesthetic using an electrical current of 50–400 joules.

If the situation is not so urgent and there is at least a few hours before problems will develop, it is customary to use intravenous infusions of an anti-arrhythmic drug to normalise the rhythm. For supraventricular tachycardias this would be intravenous Adenosine, Verapamil or Amiodarone, and for ventricular arrhythmias this would be intravenous Lignocaine or Flecainide. For long term control of arrhythmias, similar drugs are used, although Lignocaine is only available in intravenous form.

If all fails with anti-arrhythmic agents, it is possible to insert a pacemaker which delivers electric shock, rather like a DC cardioversion but from inside the heart. A small current is used, although it can sometimes be perceived as uncomfortable by the patients. In life-threatening situations, however, this can be very successful. Unfortunately it is also expensive. Such pacemakers may cost up to £17,000.

The other alternative is to try and destroy one of the accessory pathways within the heart which is helping to maintain the circuit motion and hence the tachycardia. This can be done at an electro-physiological study, using eg either an electrical current or cryotherapy when the offending pathway is obliterated. This is a highly skilled procedure and is astonishingly successful in many cases (up to 90%).

Atrial fibrillation

This tachycardia is singled out because it is so common, and two important points must be made. In atrial fibrillation the atria are quivering and not contracting. In certain circumstances this allows a clot to form on the atrial wall which may result in an embolus and possible stroke. In these situations long term anticoagulation using warfarin must be considered.

In addition there is often a problem of rate control with atrial fibrillation. Many patients will appear to have a perfectly well controlled heart rate at rest, but after 1–2 minutes of exercise their heart rates will rise to 170–180mmHg. This means that, although they may be on apparently appropriate drugs for treatment of their arrhythmia problem, they become extremely breathless with exercise and further rate control must be made using other or added anti-arrhythmic agents, eg Digoxin and Amiodarone, or Digoxin and Sotalol.

BRADYCARDIAS

Definition

A bradycardia occurs when the heart rate drops below 50 beats per minute. Not all bradycardias are significant. Vigorous training produces a slow pulse so that the heart has more reserve, in particular for long distance running. Some Olympic athletes have a resting pulse as low as 28 beats per minute. The worry over slow heart rate, therefore, is whether it produces symptoms, and not just the presence of a low rate.

The ECG in bradycardia

There are basically two types of bradycardia that one must consider – a sinus bradycardia and that produced by various degrees of heart block. The sinus bradycardia is just an ordinarily slow pulse. While it may occur with physical training, it can occur due to heart disease and other diseases such as hypothyroidism. A very slow pulse causes a faint due to vaso-vagal stimulation.

Heart block is a situation where there is either a partial or complete block in the AV node or the bundle of His which conveys the electricity from the top to the bottom of the heart (see Figure 29, page 88).

First degree block is where there is a short delay of perhaps 40–60ms down the bundle of His. Second degree 'Wenchbach' block is where the P-R interval gradually lengthens during a series of complexes until a QRS complex is dropped. Full second degree block is where there are two atrial P-waves prior to each QRS complex. A complete heart block is where there is complete

Figure 29. First degree heart block and its ECG (bottom). Depolarisation is delayed in the region of the AV node. Although the P-wave is normal there is a delay before the QRS complex appears. The PR interval (beginning of the P-wave to the beginning of the QRS complex) is greater than 0.22sec (5.5 little squares).

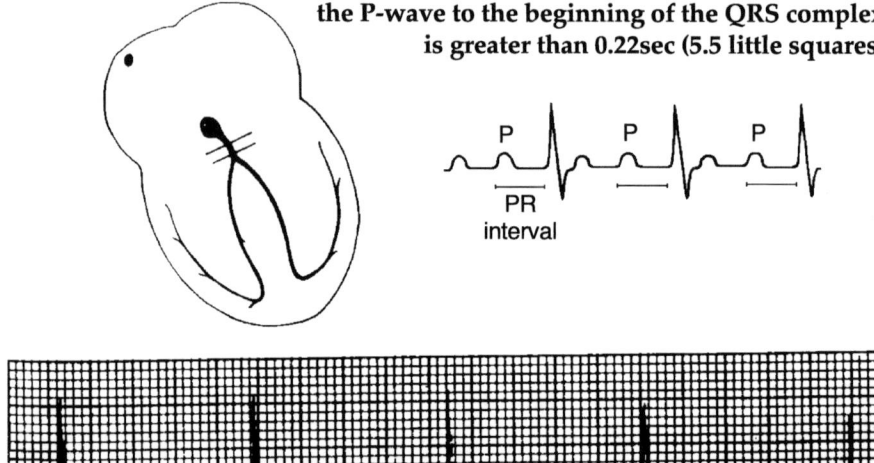

dissociation of the P-waves and QRS complexes because there is no conduction whatever down the bundle of His.

Symptoms

A significantly slow pulse will result in light headedness, dizziness, funny turns and blackouts. However, there is a particular form of blackout associated with complete heart block known as a Stokes-Adams attack (named after two Irish physicians). In complete heart block there is often a sudden cessation of the ventricular rate, causing a patient to blackout without the slightest warning. For example, this may occur when a patient is crossing the road and an injury is likely. This sudden nature of the blackout helps to distinguish it from neurological problems and other forms of arrhythmia.

Signs

The pulse will be slow, sometimes regular and sometimes irregular, with occasionally long pauses where there may be no ventricular activity at all. A curious shooting venous wave, known as a Cannon wave, will be seen in the neck of patients with complete heart block.

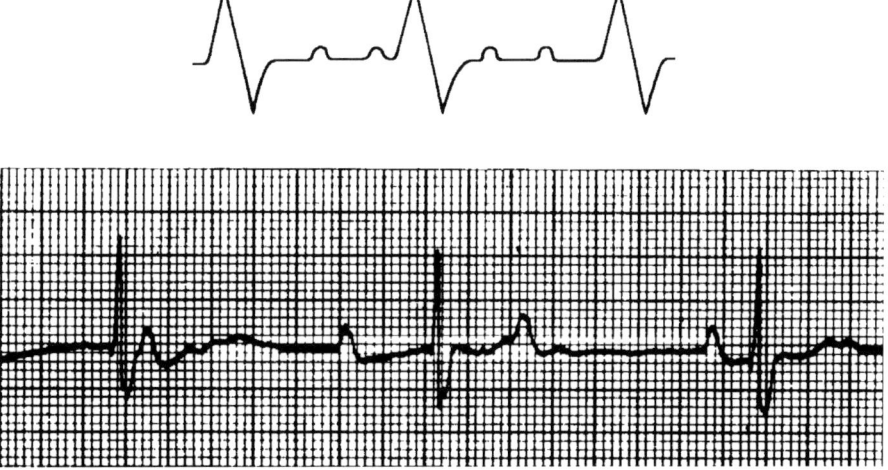

Figure 30. Complete heart block.

Block complete

Atrial activity

Ventricular activity

These two tracings combine to give the following:

Investigations

Frequent ECGs, event recorders, 24 hour tapes and all hospital monitoring may be necessary to catch bradycardias. In difficult cases an electro-physiological study may demonstrate conduction delays in the bundle of His.

Figure 31. The temporary pacemaker.

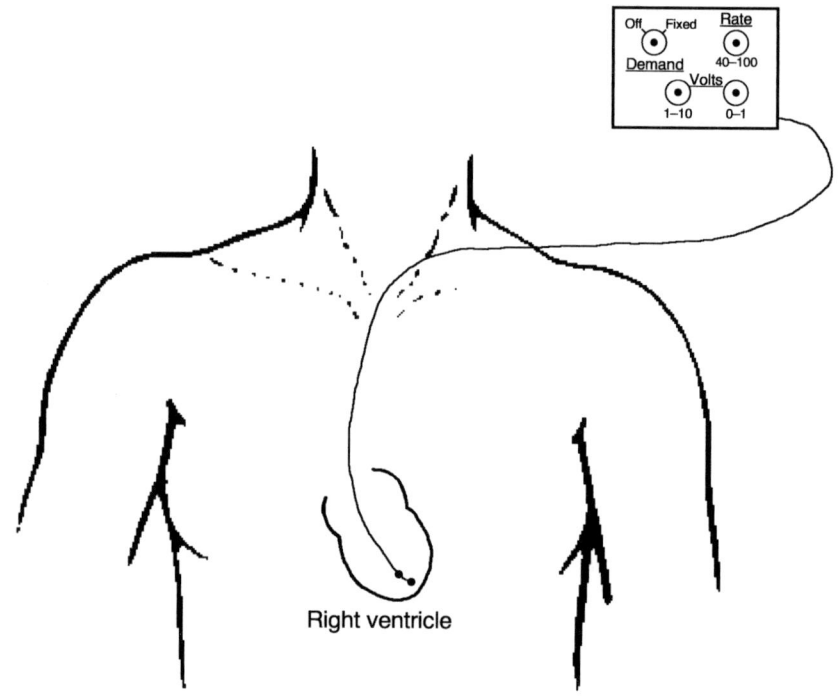

Treatment

Slow pulses will need no treatment unless they cause symptoms. There are no drugs available for speeding up the heart rate and the only treatment, therefore, is a pacemaker. In an emergency situation, a temporary pacemaker wire is inserted just above or beneath the clavicle and guided into the apex of the right ventricle by X-ray control (Figure 31). A pacemaker box is attached and usually set at 3 volts and approximately 70 beats per minute. This can be rapidly inserted in an emergency situation and is life saving. For obvious reasons it cannot be used on a permanent basis.

Practical, permanent pacemakers were developed in the 1960s. They contained nickel-cadmium batteries which lasted about two years. The pacemakers were quite bulky. With the advent of lithium batteries, small pacemakers lasting up to 10 years are now commonly used. The average modern pacemaker is about the size of an old English pocket watch. The pacemaker electrode is inserted through the cephalic vein beneath the shoulder, and the pacemaker box placed under the skin and on top of the muscle. Pacemakers are usually inserted underneath the left shoulder to avoid problems, such as when shooting.

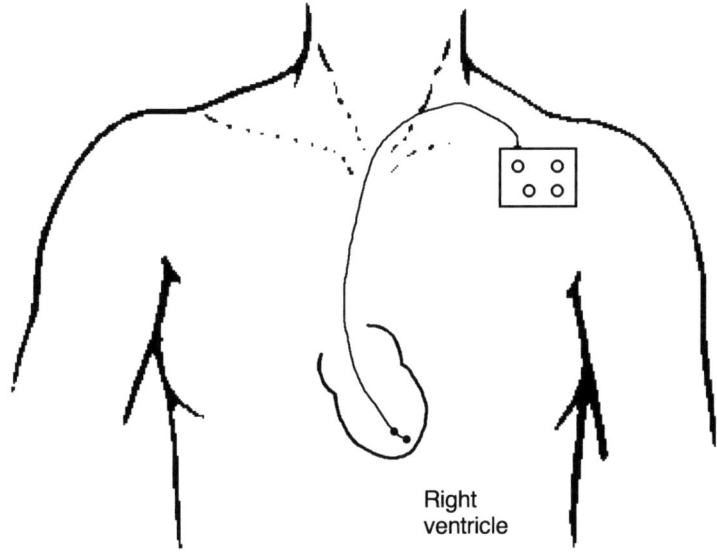

Right
ventricle

Figure 32. Unipolar (above) and bipolar (below) pacemakers.

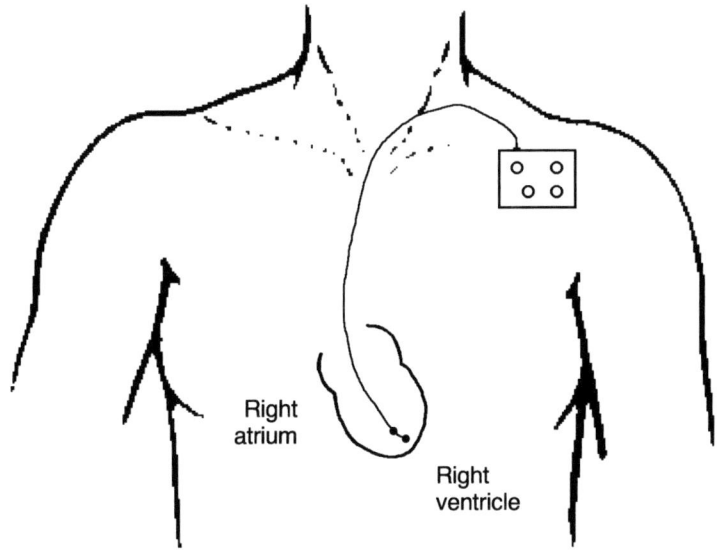

Right
atrium

Right
ventricle

Pacemakers are now very common, very clever and occasionally very expensive. There are two basic types of pacemaker (Figure 32, page 91). In one type there is a single electrode inserted into the ventricle. This stimulates the heart and also senses any occasional natural heart beat which then inhibits the pacemaker. This prevents competing rhythms from two pacemaker sources which result in palpitations and confusion. For physiological reasons, these pacemakers are not as successful as bipolar pacemakers. These pacemakers have one electrode inserted into the atrium and the other into the ventricle. They pace the two chambers in sequence, one after the other, producing a much more natural heart activity. There are less side effects with this method, but they are more expensive (£600 as opposed to £2,500).

Pacemakers have now reached the stage where they can be programmed via computers from outside the chest through the skin. It is possible for example to alter the rate at which the pacemaker fires, simply by placing a computer directly over the pacemaker box. Pacemakers have become multifunctional and, although very expensive, can be extremely useful. If the patient has a pacemaker inserted, the life of the battery and the various characteristics of the pacemaker should be checked one month after insertion and then subsequently at yearly intervals, although more frequently towards the end of the life of the pacemaker. As the batteries gradually decline, one can elect when to replace the pacemaker with a new one and avoid the problems of the patient having a failed pacemaker. Checking a pacemaker is a very simple procedure and is done in almost all district general hospitals.

CHAPTER TWELVE

VALVULAR HEART DISEASE

INTRODUCTION

There are many early descriptions of abnormal valves dating from the 17th century, all taken from dead bodies. It was the stethoscope which enabled doctors to diagnose valve lesions during life. The stethoscope was introduced in 1819 by Laennec, a Frenchman, who became convinced that only if a heart was abnormal would it produce different sounds from normal. This is why he believed angina was not related to the heart.

In 1832, James Hope of Dublin wrote a textbook describing, *inter alia*, murmurs caused by valve lesions. His descriptions are astonishingly accurate and, in the days before cardiac investigations were possible, were all that was available for diagnosis.

Although there are four heart valves, only two are relevant in day to day cardiology, the aortic and mitral valves. It is uncommon to have to repair or replace the tricuspid or pulmonary valves. As the aortic and mitral valves are subjected to much higher pressure and involve the circulation into the body rather than the lungs, they are much more likely to affect the patient symptomatically. For practical purposes, therefore, this chapter will deal largely with mitral and aortic valve disease.

PATHOPHYSIOLOGY

In the majority of cases there are two basic changes which can occur to a heart valve, ie stenosis or incompetence. If the valve is stenosed, it means that the orifice size is reduced and blood has difficulty getting through the valve. This creates a back pressure behind it and leads to less flow around the body. When the valve is incompetent, it means that it does not close properly. This allows blood to regurgitate through it and again causes a reduction in flow around the body (see Figure 33, page 94).

Although the commonest lesions are stenosis or regurgitation of the aortic or mitral valves, there is another form of valve problem affecting the mitral valve only, usually known as the billowing mitral leaflet syndrome. In this particular case, one cusp of the valve is affected and becomes much larger than the other (see Figure 34, page 94). Initially, the valve just billows back into the left atrium and causes no problems, but with time the valve cusp billows back into the left atrium and causes mitral regurgitation, which can be severe.

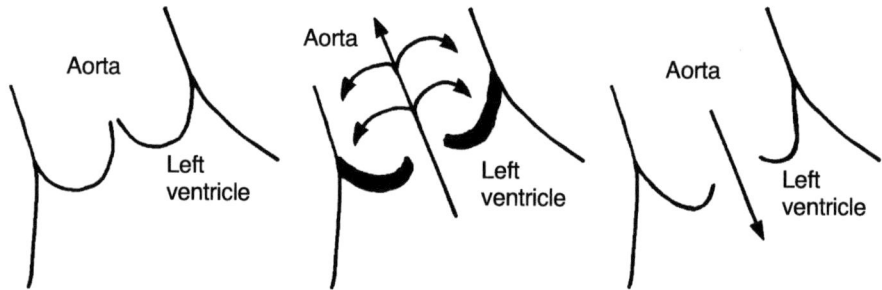

Figure 33. Valvular stenosis and regurgitation. Left: a normal aortic valve. Centre: aortic stenosis. Right: aortic regurgitation.

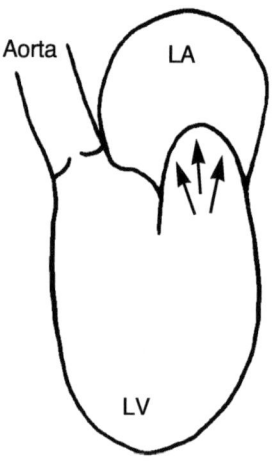

Figure 34. The billowing mitral leaflet syndrome.

Stage one (left): billowing of the leaflet only, no mitral incompetence.

Stage two (below left): billowing of the leaflet and mild/moderate mitral incompetence.

Stage three (below right): billowing of the leaflet and severe mitral incompetence.

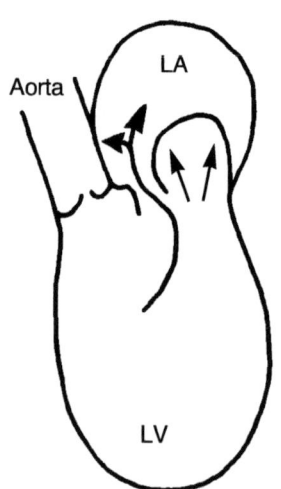

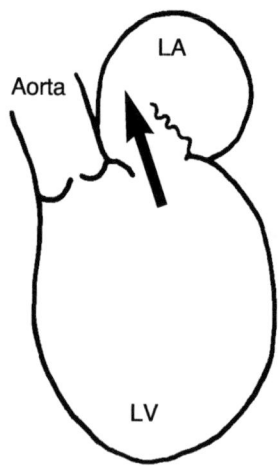

Although the commonest cause of aortic and mitral valve lesions used to be rheumatic fever, this is now rare in this country and the majority of valves become damaged either as a result of a congenital malformation or of degenerative disease of some description, in particular ischaemic heart disease.

An abnormality of the aortic valve, which has two cusps instead of three, is frequently congenital, leading to aortic stenosis and later regurgitation. The mitral valve suffers much more from ischaemic heart disease when its supports can be damaged, eg by a myocardial infarction. Mitral regurgitation then occurs. The causes of billowing mitral leaflet syndrome can be extremely varied, although the majority are congenital in origin. It probably affects about 2% of the population in this country – more females than males – although in Zulus it occurs in about 10% of the population.

SYMPTOMS

The main symptom with any valve disease is breathlessness associated with tiredness. With mitral valve disease there is the additional chance of palpitations because such patients are more likely to develop atrial fibrillation than those with aortic valve disease. Once the valve lesion has become significant, congestive heart failure follows and the patient develops swollen ankles.

Aortic stenosis is a slightly different lesion in the sense that it results in the three As – angina, attacks of unconsciousness, and asthma (cardiac). Aortic stenosis prevents adequate flow down the coronary arteries which is why it causes chest pains in addition to breathlessness, etc.

SIGNS

The major sign of valvular heart disease is the murmur. The exact details are unnecessary in such a book as this, but it takes a lot of practice to diagnose with a stethoscope. Whilst it is quite easy to hear murmurs, it is not so easy to diagnose them and assess their severity unless the doctor is experienced. This is not to denigrate the majority of doctors, but simply to point out that it is an art form acquired only by listening to murmurs more or less every day.

In addition to murmurs which may be either systolic or diastolic depending on the valve lesion, a number of confirmatory signs will be present according to the actual lesion concerned. However, it must be pointed out that the majority of confirmatory signs are only present when valvular disease is significant, and are likely to be picked up otherwise by chance. For example, in aortic stenosis the pulse can be slow rising because of the degree of restriction within the aorta. However, this will only be present when the valve is either moderately or severely affected. An abnormal heart rhythm, ie atrial fibrillation, often accompanies mitral valve disease, but again not until its later stages.

INVESTIGATIONS

Initially a chest X-ray and ECG is usually performed on patients with heart murmurs, but they are of limited value. A chest X-ray may show an enlarged heart or perhaps an enlarged left atrium along with heart failure, but will not give a diagnosis of a specific lesion. An ECG will show enlargement of chambers and perhaps strain upon the heart, but again will not give a direct diagnosis of a murmur.

The echo Doppler technique of examining the heart is of the greatest value in diagnosing heart lesions and their degree of damage. From the echo Doppler, the gradient across a valve can be measured and the valve area can be calculated in regurgitation. The degree of regurgitation can also be assessed by the Doppler technique. Whilst the echo Doppler can give fairly accurate diagnosis of valve disease, it is nearly always necessary for a patient to have a cardiac catheter before an operation could be performed. The reason for this is that one must seek evidence of co-existing ischaemic heart disease, as well as remembering that the cardiac catheterisation is the gold standard test for heart disease and will give an even more accurate diagnosis of valvular stenosis and regurgitation than the echo Doppler technique.

THE NATURAL HISTORY OF VALVE LESIONS

This can be divided into two: aortic stenosis and other valve lesions.

Aortic stenosis

Aortic stenosis has been separated out because it needs careful attention. Patients are often asymptomatic for years and then suddenly deteriorate. The symptoms (the three As) suddenly develop, and the outlook from an attack of unconsciousness to death, for example, is two years, even if no other symptoms develop. If acute left ventricular failure develops with aortic stenosis, an aortic valve replacement is required as an emergency (Figure 35).

The other valve lesions

These include aortic regurgitation and mitral regurgitation, mitral stenosis and billowing mitral leaflet syndrome.

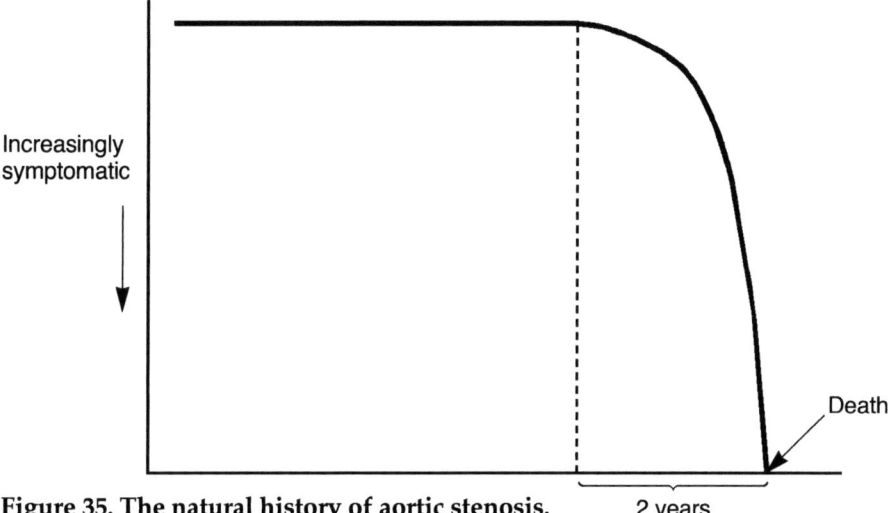

Figure 35. The natural history of aortic stenosis.

In these valve lesions, symptoms gradually develop over a period of years. There is often a sudden worsening of symptoms when the patient goes into atrial fibrillation, although this can be improved by drug treatment. Therefore, the decision to change from medical to surgical treatment can be taken at some leisure as the patient gradually develops increasing symptoms. The commonest symptoms are dyspnoea and fatigue. As a rule of thumb, if the patient on medical treatment cannot get up a flight of stairs without stopping, he needs a valve replacement (Figure 36).

Figure 36. Natural history of mitral valve disease and aortic incompetence.

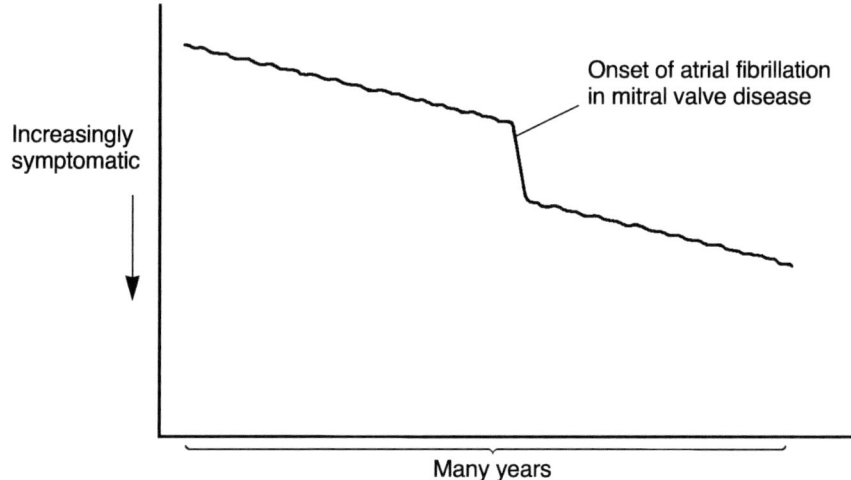

The medical treatment of valve disease

Valve disease of any kind produces three basic problems: heart failure, arrhythmias and pulmonary hypertension.

Pulmonary hypertension cannot be dealt with medically in any way whatsoever. Heart failure is dealt with by diuretics, Digoxin and either an ACE inhibitor or a vasodilator; this would be used routinely in the treatment of valve disease. Arrhythmias are dealt with medically as well, eg Digoxin for atrial fibrillation. It must be emphasised that there is no medical treatment that will affect the valve itself and correct the underlying problem, nor is there any treatment that will reverse pulmonary hypertension.

With mitral valve disease there is an increased risk of an embolus arising from the left atrium, especially when stenosis is present. The risk increases once atrial fibrillation develops and, as a general rule of thumb, patients who have mitral valve disease are anticoagulated once they reach the age of approximately 40.

SURGICAL TREATMENT

This consists of valvotomy, valve replacement and, very rarely, balloon valvuloplasty.

Valvotomy

Valvotomy consists of splitting the valve along the line of its cusps in order to open it up, and therefore can only be used for stenosis of the valve, in particular mitral stenosis. Also, it can only be used on a valve which is fairly pliable. If a valve is heavily calcified and stiff, the only effect of valvotomy would be to create gross mitral regurgitation. It is, therefore, useful in younger patients and is frequently used in third world countries where rheumatic fever is still common and patients present at a much younger age than in the UK.

Mortality of valvuloplasty is lower than mitral valve replacement at about 1–3%, and the 10 year survival following valvotomy is usually about 90%. However, 20% of patients who have mitral valvotomy will require mitral valve replacement after 10 years.

Valve replacement

It is only possible to operate upon heart valves using a heart-lung machine. This also applies to coronary artery bypass grafting.

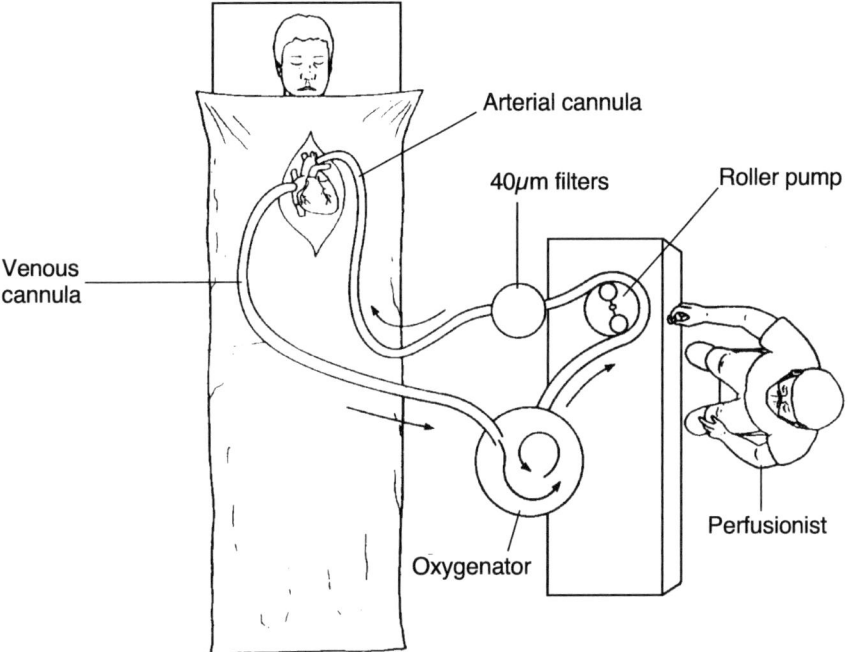

Figure 37. The heart-lung machine. A 1.5cm dia. pipe drains all the patient's blood from the venous circuit to a reservoir, from where it runs through an oxygenator. It is pressurised by the roller pump and driven through a filter before being returned to the arterial circulation through a 1cm dia. pipe.

Because the heart is in continuous motion it is difficult to operate upon unless it is 'paralysed' for a period of time. If the heart does stop functioning, blood will not perfuse the brain and the patient will be dead in a few minutes. In addition, opening up the heart allows air into the blood vessels. Such air 'emboli' would block blood flow and irreparably damage organs such as the brain. The pumping of blood around the body must therefore take place using artificial means, ie the heart-lung machine. This procedure is known as 'cardiopulmonary bypass'.

Cardiopulmonary bypass is instituted by removing venous blood from the right side of the heart, oxygenating it and pumping it back under pressure into the left side of the heart. In practice blood is taken from the vena cava or right atrium and pumped back into the aorta (see Figure 37). The surgeon puts the patient on 'bypass' and the pump technician maintains an adequate flow and pressure. To preserve the heart muscle an additional cannula is placed in the rest of the aorta beneath the cross clamp, and 'cardioplegic' solution, consisting of sodium, potassium, magnesium, calcium, chlorides and procaine, is run into the coronary arteries. This prevents the heart muscle from becoming damaged during bypass.

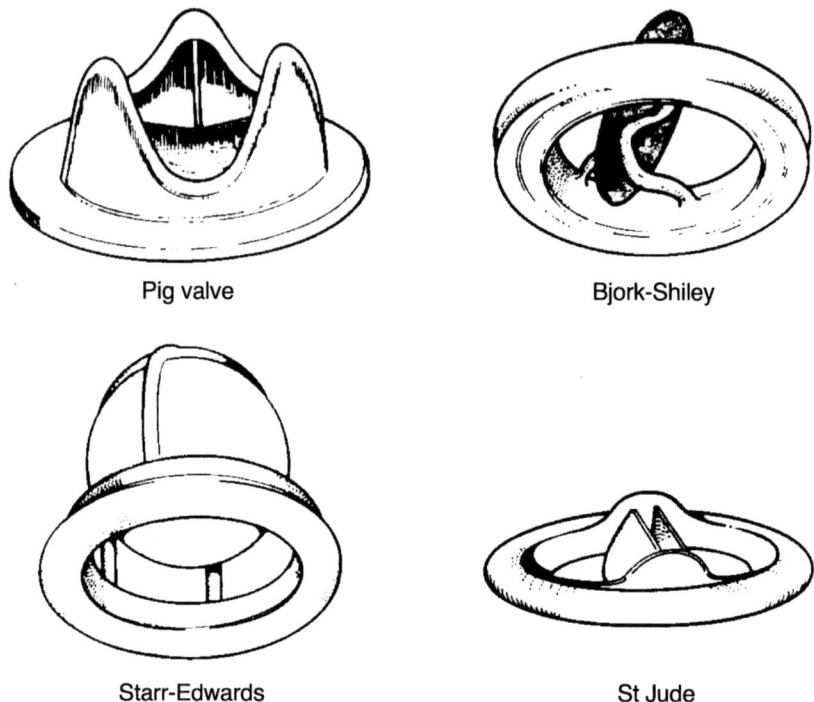

Pig valve   Bjork-Shiley

Starr-Edwards   St Jude

Figure 38. Types of prosthetic heart valve.

There are three types of prosthetic valves which are commonly used for valve replacement (see Figure 38, page 100).

The earliest type of valve was the Starr-Edwards valve, which has always been robust but is liable to clotting if the blood is not anticoagulated. It causes a mild degree of stenosis because the ball partially obstructs blood flow.

There are two types of tilting disc valves commonly in use: one is the Bjork-Shiley prosthesis, a single tilting disc valve; and the other is the St Jude valve, a double disc valve. Again these are robust and cause less obstruction to flow than the ball and cage valve, but also require anticoagulation.

The only natural type of valve used is either a heterograft or homograft valve using natural tissue on a supporting stent. The advantage of these grafts is that they do not necessarily require anticoagulants, although many centres still anticoagulate patients who have this type of valve put in the mitral position. The big disadvantage of the more natural valves is that after 10 years the majority are either stenosed or incompetent. This is due to calcification and scarring within the tissue valves.

In aortic valve replacement the mortality varies between 2–8% depending on the centre, but perhaps more significantly related to the degree of left ventricular dysfunction. If the left ventricle is tired, the mortality will clearly be higher. The five year survival for aortic valve replacement for either stenosis or regurgitation is approximately 85%. Mitral valve replacement for mitral stenosis carries a 10 year survival of 70%, whilst mitral regurgitation carries a five year survival of 70%. The difference is predominantly due to the effect of mitral regurgitation on left ventricular function which can be severe. The operative mortality for mitral valve replacement in mitral stenosis is 1–4% and for mitral regurgitation 2–8%.

Occasionally a mitral valve can be repaired. If, for example, one of the leaflets has become too large, with resulting mitral regurgitation, it can be re-shaped and sutured to approximate towards the normal. The operative risk for mitral valve repair is about half that of mitral valve replacement and, therefore, is often considered in younger patients. However, the chances are quite high that, at some later stage afterwards, the patient will need a valve replacement.

Occasionally a balloon valvuloplasty is performed. This is simply where a balloon is inserted into the aorta and inflated across the stenotic valve. Results of this procedure are not particularly good and will only be successful if the valve is pliable. Valvuloplasty is occasionally done in children to prevent a valve having to be replaced at too early an age, but this is a rare situation.

Age is normally no barrier to aortic valve replacement for aortic stenosis, but after a biological age of approximately 75 the risk increases markedly for other valve lesions.

COMPLICATIONS OF SURGICAL TREATMENT

It is extremely rare for a valve either to fracture or fail, although this has occurred once in recent years due to defective welding. There have been a number of medico-legal actions, but they are excessively rare and the makers of valves usually take the utmost care.

After the operation it is possible for the sutures to become loose or rupture around the valve causing para-valvular regurgitation. Occasionally infection of the sutures of the valve can occur, resulting in infective endocarditis.

Despite appropriate anticoagulation, occasional cases of clotting in a prosthetic valve can occur. Because patients will be on anticoagulants there will be a small risk of bleeding in both the immediate and long term post-operative period.

During 'bypass' the arterial pressure created by the heart-lung machine is about 50mmHg, ie less than half of normal. Neurological complications can occur in about 2% of patients as a result of this, eg stroke.

FOLLOW-UP AFTER VALVE REPLACEMENT

After valve replacement, patients usually return home in 7–10 days. It will take them approximately three months to return completely to normal again, although the speed of recovery is related to some extent to the left ventricular function. If the ventricle is tired, the return to normal is much slower.

The patient will be prescribed anticoagulants if that is deemed appropriate, but may also be given some anti-failure treatment which will have been used prior to the operation The replacement of the valve does not directly correct left ventricular dysfunction although this will gradually improve with time, as will pulmonary hypertension.

MEDICO-LEGAL POINTS

The waiting list

Over a number of years patients have died on the waiting list for a valve replacement. This is deeply distressing to all concerned and many factors may be involved. Each case must be discussed in its own merits.

Aortic stenosis

Aortic stenosis can be a difficult area. Generally speaking the longer the heart murmur the tighter the aortic stenosis, and therefore it is theoretically reasonably easy to assess its severity by auscultation. However, when heart failure supervenes, the left ventricle becomes so tired it cannot pump blood vigorously through the aortic valve. The consequence of this is that the murmur becomes shorter and quieter. This could be misinterpreted as only left ventricular failure and not related to valve problems. Occasionally the murmur is so quiet that it is not heard at all and the aortic stenosis is only discovered at post-mortem

One must also emphasise that, if a patient develops acute left ventricular failure with aortic stenosis, an operation will probably be needed within 24 hours or death will be highly likely. The sudden deterioration of patients with aortic stenosis can catch one unawares, so that the natural history of this lesion must always be kept in mind.

Systolic murmurs

Because aortic stenosis and mitral regurgitation are systolic murmurs, they can be dismissed as innocent murmurs, especially if they are quiet. If there is any doubt about a murmur, it must be investigated in a cardiology department.

Anticoagulants

Failure to anticoagulate a patient with mitral stenosis can result in an embolus and stroke. It is always difficult to be certain exactly when such a patient should be anticoagulated in this situation. The reason that the age of about 40 is normally suggested to begin anticoagulation is because it is about this time that patients go into atrial fibrillation, which markedly increases the risk of embolus. In females, where warfarin is contraindicated in pregnancy, anticoagulation is considered after child bearing age.

Age

Age alone is sometimes given as a reason for not operating upon a patient with valvular heart disease. This is not appropriate for the patient with aortic stenosis. It is a remarkably good operation for patients up to 80 years of age or more, with a relatively low operative mortality. The age factor becomes important with other valve lesions (MS, MR, AR) because the left ventricle is always compromised to some degree. In this situation a biological age of 75 is regarded as the upper limit of valve replacement.

Timing of valve replacement

It is generally accepted that the timing of a valve replacement is difficult, and there are many differing views on this subject. This, therefore, becomes a difficult area medico-legally.

Calcific emboli

Occasionally, small calcific emboli can detach from an aortic valve lesion. This is exceptionally rare, but arose in one particular medico-legal case. The patient argued that he ought to have had an aortic valve replacement earlier to prevent such an episode happening. However, such an occurrence of an embolus in this situation is so rare that it would not justify valve replacement purely for that reason.

Artificial valves

It must be accepted that there is no such thing as a perfect artificial heart valve, although mechanically they are constructed with the utmost care. Welding problems have occurred in a small series of Bjork-Shiley valves, but this only affected a small group of patients over a short period of time. It must be emphasised that mechanical failure of a prosthetic valve is excessively rare.

Additional ischaemic heart disease

Many older patients requiring valve replacement will also have ischaemic heart disease. Because a second thoracotomy is a hazardous procedure, one usually elects to do coronary artery bypass grafting at the same time as valve replacement if it appears to be necessary. This will inevitably increase the risk at operation although not greatly. Following any heart operation there is a lot of scarring behind the sternum with adhesions to the pericardium and surrounding tissues. At re-operation these will have to be carefully dissected; this is done at increased risk.

Quality of life

The quality of life after valve replacement is usually markedly improved. Valve replacement for aortic stenosis usually results in the patient being virtually normal. However, valve replacement for other lesions cannot be expected to be fully successful. This is because, over the years, problems such as pulmonary hypertension develop which cannot be fully reversed by an operation. Whilst improvement is generally good, one must be realistic about just how much better the patient will become.

Multiple valve replacement

Double and triple valve replacements are performed, but this increases the risk accordingly. The risks are roughly additive with the mortality at approximately 4% per valve.

Clots on artificial valves

Because of the risks of a prosthetic valve clotting up, anticoagulation is usually carefully controlled at a higher range than for other clotting problems. This necessarily increases the risk of bleeding, eg from injury. The frequency of a significant bleed requiring blood transfusion in this situation is about 1.5% per annum.

Success of a unit

Generally, there is a relationship between the success of a unit and the number of operations it performs. Centres with the best results are usually undertaking more than 500 open heart procedures each year.

CHAPTER THIRTEEN

CONGENITAL HEART DISEASE

The overall picture of congenital heart disease has changed. Many more patients are progressing to adult life with both treated and untreated congenital heart disease compared with a few years ago. Before the years of antibiotics in particular, patients with congenital heart disease were blue or cyanosed, and seldom lived beyond the age of about 20. Now many patients, even with quite severe congenital heart disease, can live into their 50s and 60s.

The overall incidence of congenital heart disease is 8 per 1,000 live births. The commonest type is the ventricular septal defect at approximately 2 per 1,000 births. A mother giving birth to a child with congenital heart disease has increased risk in future pregnancies of approximately three fold, 25 per 1,000 live births, but this is not a big risk as such. In the last 25 years there has been an enormous improvement in the ability to operate upon congenital heart disease, starting with the advent of the heart lung machine. Mortality from operations soon after birth is quite high (up to 10%), but after the first year of life becomes remarkably low. There is no doubt that the abilities of the cardiac surgeons in this field are quite remarkable.

The most difficult area of congenital heart disease is during the neonatal period where tiny and often premature babies present with possible congenital lesions. The diagnosis of these is a highly skilled procedure by paediatric echocardiographic cardiologists or by cardiac catheterisation. The degree of difficulty of cardiac catheterisation in this group is highlighted by the fact that the heart wall is as soft as the inside of a grape. Cardiac catheterisation, therefore, includes some danger and can be frightening. Congenital heart disease can be divided into neonatal, childhood and adulthood, because different types of congenital heart disease would present at these ages.

TYPES OF CONGENITAL HEART DISEASE

There is a generalised distinction between cyanotic and acyanotic congenital heart disease. Cyanosis is the desaturation with the child appearing cyanosed or blue. Cyanotic congenital heart disease is, therefore, very serious because it represents the re-routing through the heart of blood which has not been oxygenated. Because cyanotic congenital heart disease is much more serious, it is the common type of congenital heart disease in the neonatal period, ie soon after birth. The main types of cyanotic congenital heart disease all begin with the letter T: tetralogy of Fallot; transposition of the main vessels; truncus arteriosus; and tricuspid atresia. The incidence of acyanotic and cyanotic congenital heart disease is shown in Table 5.

Fortunately, acyanotic heart disease is much more common than cyanotic heart disease. Whilst cyanotic heart disease presents predominantly in neonates, acyanotic heart disease will become more apparent in small children. Cyanotic heart disease does not commonly progress through to adulthood, but can do so, and the commonest types of congenital heart disease in adulthood are ASDs, PDAs and stenosis of aortic and pulmonary valves.

Acyanotic	Atrial septal defect (ASD)	30.5%
	Ventricular septal defect (VSD)	9.8%
	Patent ductus arteriosis (PDA)	9.7%
	Pulmonary stenosis	6.9%
	Coarctation of the aorta	6.8%
	Aortic stenosis	6.1%
Cyanotic	Tetralogy of Fallot	5.8%
	Transposition of the great arteries	4.2%
	Truncus arteriosus	2.2%
	Tricuspid artesia	1.3%
All others		16.5%

Table 5. Congenital heart diseases and their incidence.

CAUSE OF CONGENITAL HEART DISEASE

The vast majority of patients with congenital heart disease have no known cause whatsoever. In only a very small percentage of cases is a cause apparent. Down's syndrome and mongolism is associated in 90% of occasions with either an ASD, VSD or tetralogy of Fallot, and another chromosomal abnormality called Turner's disease has a 20% incidence of ASD. Marfan's disease, where the patient is born very tall and slim, is associated with congenital aortic and mitral regurgitation.

Acquired congenital heart disease may occur through maternal rubella (German measles) when a PDA or pulmonary or aortic stenosis may occur; alcoholism, where VSD may occur; and with the substances such as thalidomide and lithium. There is a large list of possible causes, but emphasis must be laid on the fact that the majority have absolutely no known cause.

SPECIFIC TYPES OF CONGENITAL HEART DISEASE

Atrial septal defect (ASD)

An ASD is where there is a communication between the right and left atria. This is often the size of an old English penny, so large that it usually creates no murmur at all. A secundum ASD occurs at the top of the atrial septum and is the simplest type presenting on its own. A primum ASD is in the lower part of the atrial septum and may often involve problems of the mitral or tricuspid valves. An operation for this condition has a low mortality – less than 0.1% (see Figure 39).

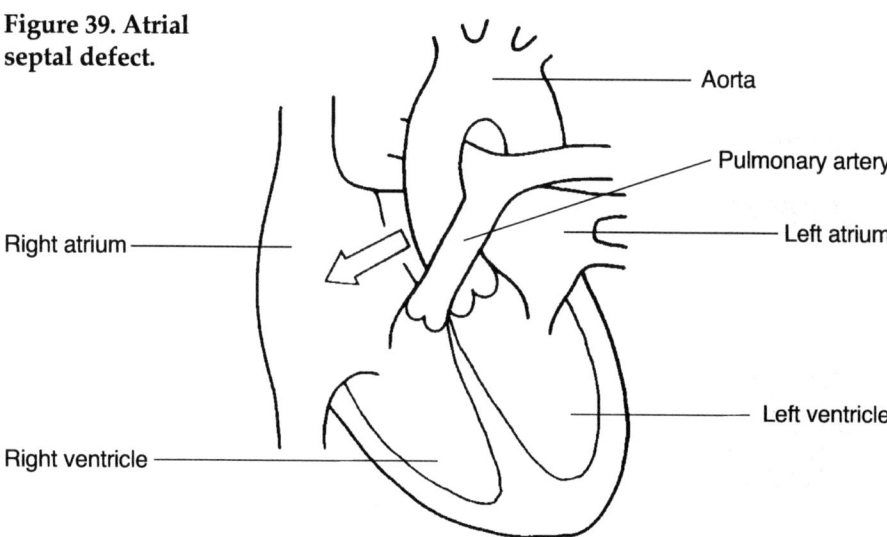

Figure 39. Atrial septal defect.

Aorta

Pulmonary artery

Right atrium

Left atrium

Left ventricle

Right ventricle

Ventricular septal defect (VSD)

This is where there is a communication between the right and left ventricles. This can be a single small hole or multiple holes like a pepper pot. It is also something that can occasionally be acquired following a myocardial infarction. Surgical closure is sometimes difficult because of the trabeculations of the ventricular septum. This is often so confusing that one may close a couple of trabeculae rather than the defect (Figure 40, page 108).

Figure 40. Ventricular septal defect.

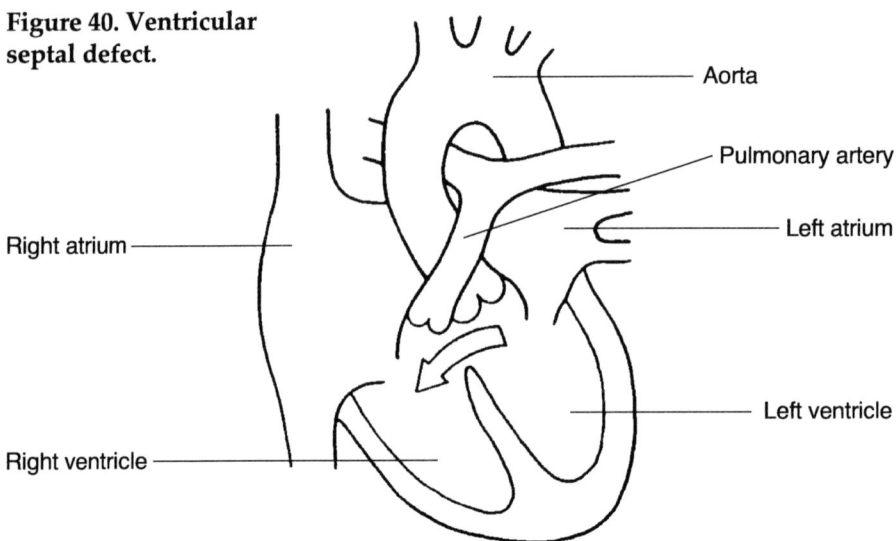

Aorta

Pulmonary artery

Left atrium

Right atrium

Left ventricle

Right ventricle

Patent ductus arteriosus (PDA)

During the gestation period of a baby, its lungs are not required. Therefore, blood circulates within the foetus from the pulmonary artery through the PDA directly into the aorta. At birth this closes naturally, but failure to do so allows a shunt from the aorta to the pulmonary artery. In premature children, indomethacin may help to close the shunt, but after birth an operation would be required (Figure 41).

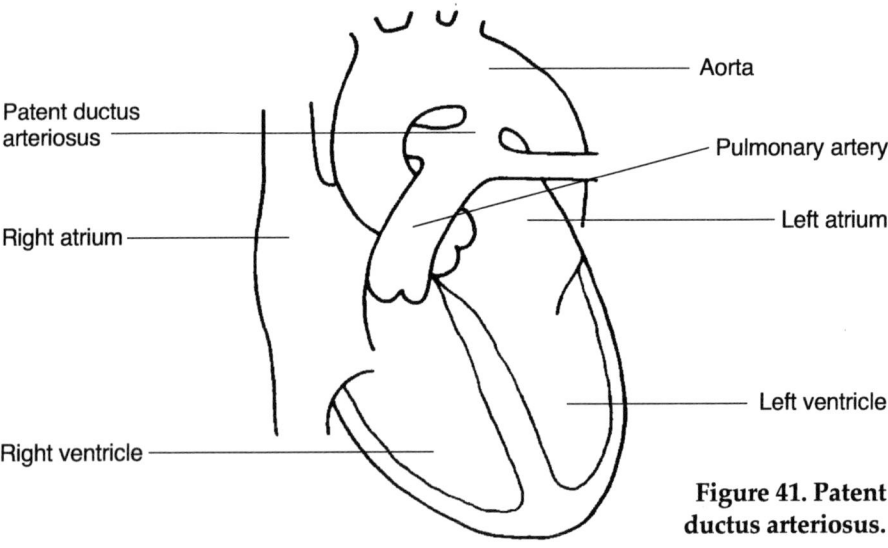

Aorta

Patent ductus arteriosus

Pulmonary artery

Left atrium

Right atrium

Left ventricle

Right ventricle

Figure 41. Patent ductus arteriosus.

Pulmonary stenosis

This lesion is not uncommon in childhood, but rarely develops in adulthood. In children it may be possible to open it up with balloon valvuloplasty rather than an operation. This is where a balloon catheter (cardiac catheterisation) is introduced across the pulmonary valve and inflated. This should split the valve across its fissures, but not damage the valve itself. Later in life a valve replacement may be necessary.

Tetralogy of Fallot

Although this was named after a Dr Fallot in the 1880s, it was described in the late 1700s by both Bailey and Farre, famous English physicians. It consists of four problems, stenosis of the pulmonary out-flow tract, an aorta over-riding into the right ventricle, a ventricular septal defect and considerable enlargement of the right ventricle. It is the commonest of the cyanotic congenital heart lesions, where blood preferentially goes into the aorta rather than the pulmonary artery and so does not get oxygenated. In children, total correction is possible, but in the neonate, a palliative operation might be necessary until the child is older (Figure 42).

**Figure 42. Tetralogy of Fallot.
LV = left ventricle; and
RV = right ventricle.**

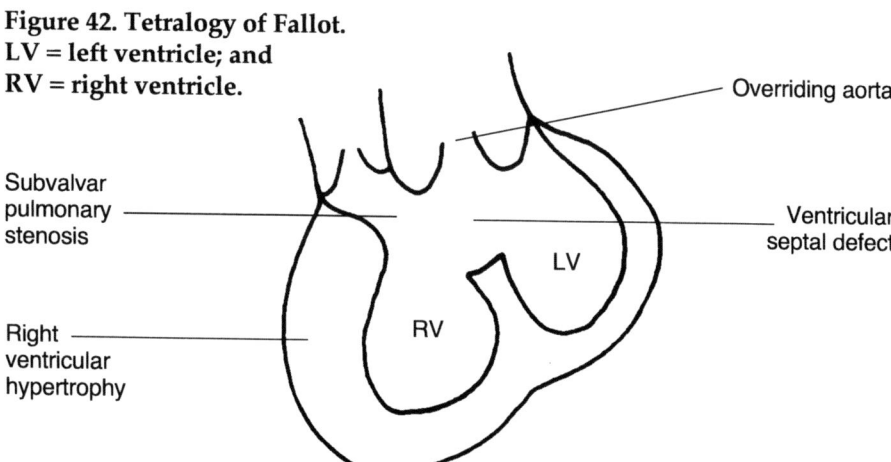

Subvalvar pulmonary stenosis

Overriding aorta

Ventricular septal defect

LV

Right ventricular hypertrophy

RV

Coarctation of the aorta

A constriction of the aorta immediately distal to the site of the ductus arteriosus can cause considerable restriction of flow to the lower aorta. The constriction may be so tight that it is only 1mm across. Blood travels by co-laterals to the lower organs and extremities, but only at the expense of a high pressure in the ascending aorta. The coarctation can be repaired by a relatively straightforward plumbing operation, but there often remains small aneurysms within the brain (Berry aneurysms) which may burst even after repair of the lesion. In addition it is not uncommon to develop arrhythmias later in life despite successful repair.

Transposition of the great vessels

This is a situation where, in effect, the aorta arises from the right ventricle and the pulmonary artery from the left ventricle. Death would be automatic without the presence of a shunt, present usually at atrial or ventricular level (see Figure 43).

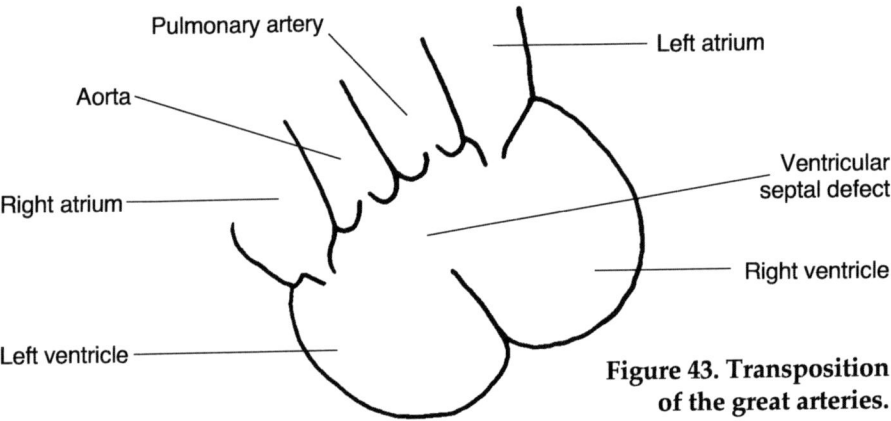

Figure 43. Transposition of the great arteries.

Truncus arteriosus

In this situation a single tube arises from both the right and left ventricles (Figure 44) which then leads into the aorta and pulmonary arteries. Like transposition of the main vessels, it is inevitably a cyanotic problem.

Tricuspid atresia

In this situation the tricuspid valve fails to develop and shunts must be present in both the atria and the ventricle for the child to survive.

PATHOLOGICAL CONSEQUENCES OF UNTREATED ACYANOTIC CONGENITAL HEART LESIONS

Pulmonary hypertension and cyanosis

In the lesions where a shunt is present (ASD, VSD, PDA) between the right and left sides of the heart, there is greatly increased flow through the right

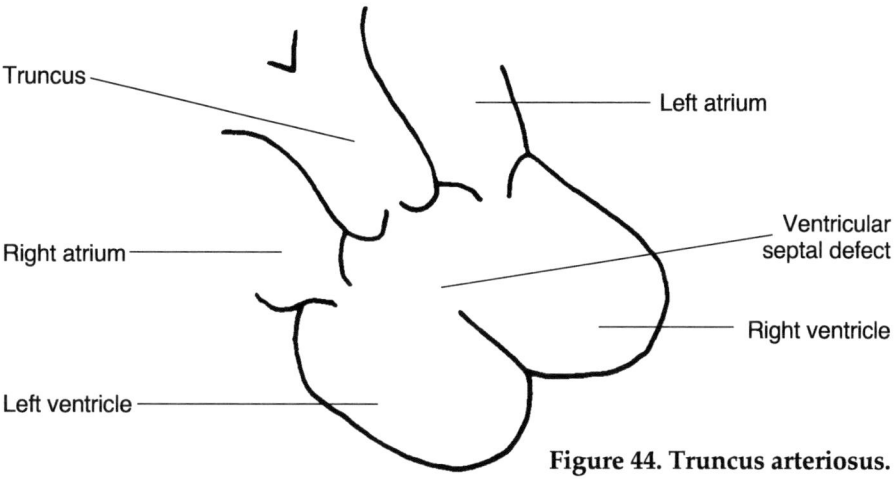

Truncus

Left atrium

Ventricular
septal defect

Right atrium

Right ventricle

Left ventricle

Figure 44. Truncus arteriosus.

ventricle and pulmonary artery. This is because the pressure in the left side of the heart is so much greater than in the right side. The flow may be 2–4 times the usual amount through the pulmonary artery. The pulmonary artery reacts to this by gradual constriction, resulting in pulmonary hypertension. In turn this leads to right ventricular hypertrophy and enlargement. Therefore, if the shunt is not closed, these problems will develop. As the pulmonary pressure increases and the pressure exceeds that in the left ventricle, the shunt reverses with deoxygenated blood pouring into the aorta. This is known as the Eisenmenger complex.

Heart failure

If untreated, the increased demand on the heart will cause heart failure. With shunts, both left and right ventricles will fail, with pulmonary stenosis the right ventricle will fail and with coarctation and aortic stenosis the left ventricle will fail. The timing of failure will depend on the severity of the lesion and is treated similarly to any other form of heart failure.

Other problems

If the lesion is severe the child may fail to thrive. Symptoms of chest pain and syncope may also occur and clubbing may develop. All lesions except a simple ASD are susceptible to infectious endocarditis.

NEONATAL PRESENTATION OF CONGENITAL HEART DISEASE

In small children, congenital heart disease presents as silent heart failure (the child has a rapid breathing rate) or cyanosis (when the child looks dusky). It must be remembered that cyanosis is common in babies, and most healthy children look blue at the edges when cold. In addition, cyanosis can be of respiratory or haematological origin in certain situations.

The commonest lesion presenting with heart failure at this age is hypoplastic left heart syndrome – where the left ventricle is tiny and underdeveloped and clearly does not function adequately. Other lesions presenting at this age causing heart failure include coarctation, aortic stenosis and truncus arteriosis. With hypoplastic left heart syndrome the only option would be a heart transplant.

PRESENTATION OF CONGENITAL HEART DISEASE IN OLDER CHILDREN

Older children will usually present with acyanotic congenital heart disease, especially ASD, VSD, PDA. The commonest cyanotic congenital heart disease will be tetralogy of Fallot.

CYANOTIC CONGENITAL HEART DISEASE PRESENTING IN ADULTS

This is now becoming much less frequent because of the ability to treat congenital heart disease in the neonatal and infancy period. However, there still exists a number of people who were born before the era of cardiac surgery and who have developed the Eisenmenger syndrome, but still manage to cope remarkably well with life even if they are breathless and susceptible to chest infections. Diagnosis in these older people is difficult and can only be done by echocardiography and cardiac catheterisation. Because of the high pulmonary artery pressure which develops in most of these patients, it is not possible to operate on any of them and correct the defect. The commonest abnormality in these elder groups is an ASD with an Eisenmenger situation. Mortality rate from the age of 40 is about 6% per annum.

OPERATING ON CONGENITAL HEART DISEASE

The current ability of surgeons to operate on congenital heart disease is remarkable, although it is fair to say that mortality under the age of six months remains high. If an operation can be postponed until the child is older it is sensible to do so. An ASD or VSD for example can often be closed when a child is five to 10 years old. Nevertheless, major reconstructive surgery correcting tetralogy of Fallot is certainly possible in young children and has a high degree of success.

Occasionally, however, the child may be too ill to cope with a major operation. In this situation it is occasionally possible to buy time by creating an additional shunt which helps to keep the oxygen saturation higher than would be normal. This can be done by operation and originally involved the right subclavian artery being anastomosed to the right pulmonary artery. This was a dramatic operation, first performed in the late 1940s when blue babies suddenly became pink. Unfortunately it is not a long lasting procedure because, eventually, pulmonary hypertension will supervene. It does, however, allow a child to grow large enough in order to have major surgery later.

Another temporising procedure is to band, ie constrict, the pulmonary arteries. This is done if it is clear that a severe shunt is causing pulmonary hypertension and it is not possible to close the original congenital lesion. By banding the pulmonary arteries one is creating effective pulmonary stenosis which protects the pulmonary arteries. Operating on congenital heart lesions requires bypass procedure in the same way as adults.

PREGNANCY AND CONGENITAL HEART DISEASE

The mortality of the mother and baby in a pregnancy with an ASD or VSD is surprisingly good, but with a lesion such as Eisenmenger syndrome the mortality is 50%. There is a wide range of mortalities from good to severe which depends entirely on the nature of the lesion and the fitness of the patient.

CHAPTER FOURTEEN

INFECTIVE ENDOCARDITIS

INTRODUCTION

Infective endocarditis is a rare but dangerous condition. There are approximately 150 cases a year in the UK and the mortality is still perhaps as high as 30%. By far the commonest type of infection is bacterial and therefore its treatment is with high dose antibiotics, but before the era of such treatment the illness was universally fatal and known as malignant endocarditis. Its importance medico-legally is that it is nearly always preventable with a short course of antibiotics but, if this fails to happen, disaster can occur.

PATHOPHYSIOLOGY

There are two essential elements required in infective endocarditis. The first is a source of bacterial or fungal infection and the second is some form of damaged or abnormal structure within the heart on which the infection can start. The infection embeds itself in this abnormal area and causes subsequent damage with swelling, fibrosis and destruction (see Figure 45). The commonest site for infectious endocarditis is a damaged heart valve, either rheumatic or congenital in origin, including a prolapsing mitral valve. It can also, however, occur in congenital heart disease and cardiomyopathies.

The effects of endocarditis are local and general.

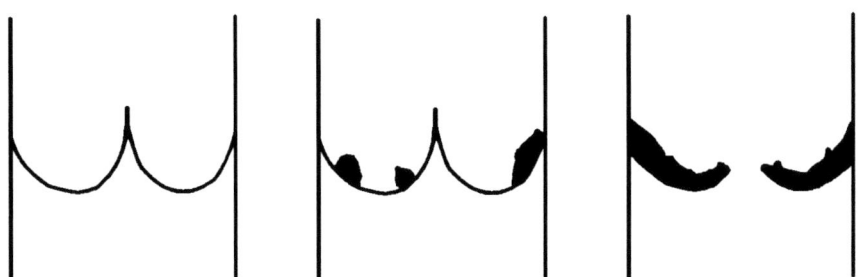

Figure 45. Infectious endocarditis on the aortic valve. Left: the normal bicuspid aortic valve. Centre: active infection on the valve cusps. Right: the fibrosed and distorted valve post-infection (valvar incompetence).

Local

The infection attacks the abnormal heart valve, creating either regurgitation or stenosis.

General

Because of the prolonged infection the patient feels unwell with a fever. Occasionally, fragments break away from the initial site of infection and become emboli which pass along the blood stream to organs such as the kidney and brain.

The commonest sources of bacteria are dental treatment, bowel operations or wounds which may become infected. The commonest bacteria to be involved is *Streptococcus* (60%) followed by *Staphylococci* (20%) and *Enterococci* (10%). In elderly people infectious endocarditis can occasionally damage a valve showing degeneration. This is most likely to occur in debilitated, chronically ill people.

CLINICAL PRESENTATION

The onset of infectious endocarditis is insidious. It comes on over several weeks with the patient noticing fatigue, weight loss, a general feeling of being ill and a fever. Because these feelings are so common in many diseases, the diagnosis will be missed unless the doctor has a high index of suspicion. Any patient who is feeling ill in this way and who is known to have heart valve disease must be considered to be at risk from endocarditis. If left untreated for several weeks, damage to the heart valve or other site will develop and give rise to emboli. Once the valve is damaged, it may become either stenosed or incompetent. This may result in heart failure which can be rapidly progressive. The presence of heart failure causes increased breathlessness and may lead to infected pulmonary oedema. Emboli may disperse to all parts of the body, but particularly in the kidney, spleen, brain and skin. Antigen antibody complexes developing as a result of the infection may lead to small apparent 'emboli' and appear eg under the fingernails as splinter haemorrhages.

The course of infective endocarditis may run over weeks or months and without antibiotics will be gradually downhill. The rapidity of progression of the illness depends on the fitness of the patient, although antibiotics usually, but not always, produce a rapid general improvement in health. Unfortunately, despite the best treatment a complete cure may not be possible and even death may occur.

DIAGNOSIS

The diagnosis will not be made unless the doctor considers the possibility of endocarditis. The most important test is the blood culture which will reveal the organism in approximately 60% of cases. If a patient has already had antibiotics, blood cultures are unlikely to be positive.

Once admitted to hospital the patient will have an echocardiograph which often shows lumps of bacteria and inflammatory material around the origin of the endocarditis.

TREATMENT

Prevention

The most vital part of treatment is prevention. All patients thought to be at risk of endocarditis are told that they must be given antibiotics should they visit the dentist, undergo operations or give birth. Table 6 (page 118) shows one of the currently recommended prophylactic procedures of prescribing antibiotics. Not every procedure performed by the dentist requires antibiotics; these are usually reserved for tooth extraction, root filling and vigorous scaling and polishing. If there is any doubt it is better to prescribe antibiotics. Any surgical operation which may become infected requires prophylactic antibiotics, the most obvious of which is an operation upon the bowel.

Active infection

Once endocarditis has been diagnosed, high dose intravenous antibiotics are required for up to six weeks. The exact course of treatment varies considerably according to the organism which is causing the problem. Fortunately *Streptococcus* is still very sensitive to penicillin but other organisms may require sophisticated antibiotics. Many cases of endocarditis may need only a fortnight's intravenous treatment followed by a few weeks of high dose oral treatment.

In cases where patients have been immunosuppressed or have been on antibiotics for a long time, it is possible to develop fungal endocarditis. This will be treated with high dose, intravenous, antifungal treatment but is more difficult to manage than bacterial endocarditis. If, during the treatment for endocarditis, the damaged valve precipitates heart failure, a valve operation may be required. At operation, all signs of the infection will be scrupulously eradicated and a prosthetic valve inserted under maximum sterility. It is

---

Standard regimen – ampicillin 2g i.v. (or i.m.) plus gentamycin 1.5mg/kg i.v. (or i.m.) (not to exceed 80mg) 30min before procedure, followed by amoxicillin 1.5g orally 6h after the dose. Alternatively, parental regimen may be repeated once 8h after initial dose.

Amoxicillin/ampicillin/penicillin-allergic patients – vancomycin 1g i.v. given over 1h plus gentamycin 1.5mg/kg i.v. (or i.m.) (not to exceed 80mg) 1h before procedure. May be repeated once 8h after initial dose.

Alternative oral regimen for low-risk patients – amoxicillin 3g orally 1h before procedure, then 1.5g hours after initial dose.

Table 6. Above: regimens for genitourinary and gastrointestinal procedures. Below: prophylactic regimens for dental, oral or upper respiratory tract procedures in patients at risk.

Standard regimen – amoxicillin 3g orally 1h before procedure, then 1.5g 6h after initial dose.

Amoxicillin/penicillin-allergic patients – erythromycin ethylsuccinate 88mg or erythromycin stearate 1g orally 2h before procedure, then half the dose 6h after initial administration; or clindamycin 300mg orally 1h before procedure and 150mg 6h after initial dose.

---

unusual to require a valve replacement in this situation, but once signs of heart failure begin to develop a patient should be transferred to a cardiac surgery unit fairly rapidly.

Special points

Endocarditis is traditionally divided into four groups:

(a) culture-positive;

(b) culture-negative;

(c) prosthetic endocarditis; and

(d) endocarditis due to intravenous drug abuse.

Culture-positive endocarditis is where the organism has been identified. This occurs in about 60% of occasions and is most likely to be the situation if the patient has not received any antibiotics before coming into hospital. Unfortunately, in the early stage of endocarditis many patients are assumed to have a chest or similar infection and will have received broad spectrum antibiotics. In this situation the cultures are likely to be negative.

When the offending organism is not known, the patient is given a broad spectrum of antibiotics in high dosage and the temperature is observed carefully. If the temperature falls fairly quickly, ie in 2–3 days, it suggests that the antibiotics are correct. If not, the antibiotics may have to be changed successively until the patient appears to be improving.

Endocarditis on a prosthetic valve is serious. On a metal valve, the infection will actually start on the sutures anchoring it to the heart. It is difficult to get high levels of antibiotics around the sutures and therefore it is almost inevitable that the valve will have to be replaced and the sutures removed. Similarly, endocarditis on a tissue valve causes relatively rapid destruction, and valve replacement must be considered if any risk develops.

Intravenous drug abusers have a different pathology. This is because infection is carried through the veins to the right side of the heart. Thus in drug abusers it will be the tricuspid and pulmonary valves which become damaged. Any release of emboli will be mopped up by the lungs and none will reach the systemic system, ie no emboli will reach the brain or kidneys. Consequently the mortality of drug abuse endocarditis is only about 10%, considerably less than that of ordinary endocarditis.

MEDICO-LEGAL POINTS

Failure of prophylaxis

In theory every case of infective endocarditis is preventable provided antibiotics are given at the appropriate time. This can never be fully achieved, but it is most important for every patient with valvular or congenital heart disease with a risk of endocarditis to be told to remind a dentist or a surgeon if some sort of appropriate procedure is required.

There must inevitably be some responsibility on the patient in this situation, especially when the dentist is not expected to be able to auscultate and diagnose valvular heart disease. The dentist should, of course, ask every patient if they have any risk of endocarditis by enquiring about valvular heart disease. This is normally done surprisingly well by all dentists.

In the hospital setting there is also some patient responsibility because it is not expected that surgeons, for example, would be able to diagnose minor degrees of valvular heart disease. As many surgical procedures are covered with antibiotics anyway, the risk of endocarditis is reduced. In theory, if a patient is admitted to their local hospital, there should be previous records indicating the presence of valvular heart disease. It cannot be over-emphasised to the 'at risk' patient just how important it is for them to remember to demand antibiotics when they undergo any procedure which might be a problem.

Failure of diagnosis

The GP sees so many patients with coughs, colds and chest infections that it is virtually impossible to remember to consider endocarditis without a high index of suspicion. Most GPs will know their patients well and, if there is any possibility of valvular heart disease, will treat them accordingly. Some patients, however, are temporary residents and others will have seldom visited their doctor, so that their past history may not be entirely clear.

It must be remembered that every time patients with a valve problem develops a flu-like illness, they probably do not have endocarditis. It clearly would be inappropriate to send every patient to hospital who has a valve lesion and a temperature. The most important feature which makes the doctor consider the diagnosis is several weeks of fatigue and feeling unwell in a known valvular heart disease patient. If there is any suspicion, the doctor should ask patients to take their temperature night and morning for a week and at the same time do blood cultures and a full blood count. If there is any concern at all the patient should be referred to the hospital for further tests including an echocardiogram.

Hospital situation

Despite the most effective antibiotics and all the care provided in hospital, disasters still occur. The focus of infection around a valve can be so dense it prevents adequate antibiotic treatment, and emboli can arise from the valve after several weeks of treatment. There are reported cases of strokes occurring after three or four weeks of intravenous antibiotic treatment.

The most important aspects of treatment are the maintenance of the intravenous antibiotics and regular examination of the patient for any signs of heart failure. Should heart failure develop, valve replacement must be considered. Because high dose antibiotics are used, adverse reactions can occasionally occur. Gentamycin is commonly used in the treatment of endocarditis, but high doses can damage the inner ear, causing dizziness and deafness. Therefore, the use of that specific antibiotic should be curtailed if there is any suspicion of these symptoms appearing.

CHAPTER FIFTEEN

CARDIOMYOPATHIES

INTRODUCTION

In medicine, cardiomyopathies are a relatively new concept, the name first being used in the late 1960s. The dominant feature of a cardiomyopathy is poor contractile function, the whole of the heart muscle being relatively equally affected. This separates it from ischaemic heart disease where the heart muscle is affected in patches, although after multiple areas of damage caused by ischaemia, the phrase ischaemic cardiomyopathy can be used.

There are two basic types of cardiomyopathy – dilated and hypertrophic (Figure 46). The dilated cardiomyopathy usually affects the left ventricle which becomes enlarged and poorly contracting.

The hypertrophic type of cardiomyopathy is the result of considerable over-growth of cardiac muscle without enlargement of the left ventricular cavity. Indeed, the muscle may encroach upon the cavity and reduce the left ventricular size. Historically, cardiomyopathies were probably thought to be 'degenerative heart disease', and both 'gouty' and 'fatty' hearts were old diagnoses probably representing dilated cardiomyopathies.

The first description of a hypertrophic cardiomyopathy was in 1966 in an article in the *British Heart Journal* where the deaths of eight young people with abnormal thickening of the left ventricular walls were described. Hypertrophic cardiomyopathy is now well known and has become a worry to young sportsmen. There is a third, rare type of cardiomyopathy called 'restrictive', when an insoluble protein such as amyloid is laid down within the cardiac muscle preventing the left ventricle relaxing.

Figure 46. The myopathies. Left: a normal left ventricle. Centre: dilated cardiomyopathy. Right: hypertrophic cardiomyopathy.

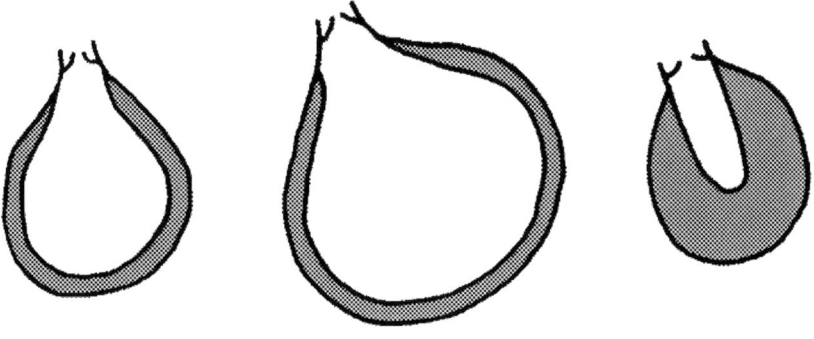

DILATED CARDIOMYOPATHY

Introduction

The majority of dilated cardiomyopathies are primary in origin, ie there is no known cause (>90%). The muscle simply dilates and contracts poorly, although the total amount of heart muscle is probably slightly increased. Secondary causes include viral, lack of thiamine (vitamin B_1), diabetes, alcohol, post-delivery, cobalt and cyclophosphamide. Despite the enormous number of possible secondary causes, very few are actually identified.

Pathophysiology

Although the total amount of heart muscle may actually increase in a dilated cardiomyopathy, all the muscle is poorly contracting. Microscopically larger myofibrils and scarring are seen, but there is nothing which can be treated directly by medication.

Symptoms and signs

The predominant problem of a cardiomyopathy is congestive cardiac failure resulting in breathlessness and fatigue. Because blood is relatively slow moving in the left ventricle, it is possible to get a thrombus on the side of the ventricular wall and emboli may detach, giving rise to problems such as a stroke. On examination the heart is enlarged and, because the ring of the mitral valve is dilated, mitral regurgitation is often present. There are no pathognomonic signs, however, which indicate a cardiomyopathy, and the diagnosis is made by investigation.

Investigations

A chest X-ray will show an enlarged heart with possible heart failure, and an ECG may show some left ventricular hypertrophy with non-specific T-wave changes, but there are no specific signs of a cardiomyopathy. It is not uncommon to find bundle branch-block patterns and often small QRS complexes throughout.

The most important means of diagnosis is the echocardiogram which shows an enlarged, poorly dilating left ventricle. It is not absolutely necessary to perform a cardiac catheterisation for this type of cardiomyopathy unless there is suspicion of coronary atheroma. Cardiac muscle biopsy does not usually help the diagnosis and has largely been abandoned.

Treatment

First, there must be the elimination of any offending cause of the cardiomyopathy, eg alcohol. Then the treatment is essentially that for congestive cardiac failure, although anticoagulation is often considered. The latter is not, however, universal and there may be a number of contraindications.

Because ACE inhibitors have been shown to improve life expectancy in patients with heart failure of this nature, it is usual for them to be prescribed provided the blood pressure is not too low. Occasionally beta-blockers can be used. By slowing the heart rate, they allow a longer filling time of the left ventricle which results in better cardiac output. However, they must be used with great caution or they may cause, or worsen, heart failure. Most patients with cardiomyopathies will probably have a 24 hour ECG tape recording. If this demonstrates arrhythmias, an anti-arrhythmic agent may be needed long term.

Finally, in younger people the possibility of surgery must be considered. End-stage cardiac failure in a patient with a cardiomyopathy who is under the age of 50 would certainly constitute a good indication for heart transplantation.

Prognosis

It is not possible to generalise on the mortality rates of cardiomyopathies because of the various types of cardiomyopathy. Some may actually improve and some may stay the same for many years.

Overall, the two year mortality is 40% and the four year mortality 60%. However, if the patient survives four years, the mortality remains fairly constant and at l0 years the mortality is 65%.

Patients who have a relative with a dilated cardiomyopathy often ask if there is any chance it is hereditary. Fortunately, familial cardiomyopathies are rare and it is usually possible to reassure the patient strongly.

HYPERTROPHIC CARDIOMYOPATHY

Introduction

The hypertrophic type of cardiomyopathy is divided into obstructive and non-obstructive. As the muscle size increases in the left ventricle problems occur during systole. When the ventricle contracts, the septum moves close to the anterior cusp of the mitral valve and causes an obstruction to the outlet. A gradient develops between the left ventricle and the aorta, increasing left ventricular strain. The non-obstructive type is the most common, when the left ventricular muscle is thickened and contract poorly, but no obstruction occurs.

Pathophysiology

In addition to the problems of systolic function there is a failure of the muscle to relax in diastole. Sometimes there is a higgledy-piggledy arrangement of the myofibrils with muscle contracting against itself. The degree of muscular thickening can range from mild to severe and can be localised to one part of the left ventricular wall, eg the septum. There are occasions also where only the right ventricle is affected.

Symptoms and signs

Breathlessness and tiredness are the main symptoms. Because the muscle outgrows its blood supply, chest pain is also common. Syncope may occur not only because of arrhythmias, but also because of the abnormal muscle function. It is syncope which presents in young athletes and creates such consternation.

Hypertrophic cardiomyopathies were thought to occur mainly in the teens and 20s, but they are now increasingly diagnosed in the elderly, indicative of the wide spectrum of the problem. On examination there may be mild cardiac enlargement and the pulses can be jerky due to outflow obstruction. The obstruction sometimes gives rise to a murmur. In many cases there will be virtually no signs at all.

Diagnosis and investigations

The first clue to a hypertrophic cardiomyopathy may be a routine ECG. This may show large left or right ventricular forces indicative of thick cardiac muscle. In addition, T-wave inversion may occur indicating strain upon the heart. In the late stages of cardiomyopathy the QRS complexes may become small, especially with severe heart failure. The diagnosis is usually made from the echocardiograph. The echo shows marked thickening of the left ventricular walls and a small left ventricular cavity. There is often a degree of asymmetrical hypertrophy within the ventricle and the anterior cusp of the mitral valve can be seen to be moving forward during systole. Cardiac catheterisation may be necessary to assess the gradient across the outflow tract of the left ventricle and in some cases it may be justifiable to do a cardiac biopsy.

Treatment

The main treatment in this condition is with beta-blockers. These help the muscles to relax, reduce its bulk and make contraction more efficient. Quite high doses, especially of Propranolol, are used with success. Occasionally calcium antagonists such as Verapamil and Diltiazem may be appropriate, and if the patient demonstrates arrhythmias on a 24 hour tape, anti-arrhythmics must be used. Very rarely an operation to relieve the obstruction or repair a mitral valve might be considered necessary.

In general, the patient should avoid strenuous sudden activity. This may cause a rapid increase in the obstruction of the outflow tract of the left ventricle due to a sudden increase in adrenaline, etc, as well as result in arrhythmias. It should also be noted that these patients may be subject to endocarditis and should receive appropriate prophylaxis.

Prognosis

In adults the overall mortality is approximately 3% per annum, but in children who often have a more severe form of HCM it is about 6% per annum. Having quoted these figures, one must be aware of the fact that HCMs represent a spectrum of disease and life expectancy may vary enormously. Perhaps the most difficult problem is identifying those patients at most risk. The younger the patient, and especially those with a family history of HCM, then the more at risk they are. In adults arrhythmias can be a marker of sudden death. The onset of atrial fibrillation is also a poor prognostic sign.

Screening

If a patient is found to have an HCM it is appropriate to screen close relatives. Brothers, sisters and children should be screened with an ECG and if there is any suspicion, an echocardiograph should be performed. If a patient has any hint of light headedness, he must also have a 24 hour ECG tape recording.

In general it is better to be on the safe side and investigate if there is any doubt. Deaths from HCMs can occur in very fit young men when the ECG may appear to show an 'athletic heart', which is perfectly normal, but also looks like a HCM. In this case an echocardiograph easily demonstrates the presence or absence of HCM.

CHAPTER SIXTEEN

MISCELLANEOUS CONDITIONS

PULMONARY HYPERTENSION

Pulmonary hypertension is a rise in the pulmonary artery pressure above approximately 30/15. This increases the pressures on the right side of the heart and puts strain on the right ventricle. It is very similar to systemic hypertension, but the problem is that there is no medical treatment which will reduce pulmonary hypertension once it has developed.

Pulmonary hypertension occurs in a number of conditions, in particular valvular heart disease, untreated congenital heart disease, recurrent pulmonary emboli and some tropical diseases, but the majority are found co-incidentally and have no known cause. The high pressure of the arteries causes stiffness in the lungs and hence a great deal of breathlessness and subsequent tiredness. On examination the right ventricle will be found to be heaving because of the increased pressure associated with a high venous pressure visible in the neck. The ECG shows right ventricular hypertrophy and the chest X-ray a narrowing of the peripheral pulmonary arteries.

If the underlying cause of the pulmonary hypertension can be treated, eg a valve replacement, pulmonary hypertension will improve but no drugs will directly reduce the pressure. In the absence of treatment the patient will progressively deteriorate and the pressure within the pulmonary arteries become so great that coughing of blood (haemoptysis) will occur, sometimes in copious quantities. Therefore, death will inevitably ensue at some stage.

PULMONARY EMBOLISM

Pulmonary emboli are clots which lodge in the pulmonary arteries. They can be small and multiple or large and dramatic. If present in any number they will inevitably result in back pressure upon the right ventricle and pulmonary hypertension will develop. If the clots are small, they may go unnoticed for some time, causing the patient to become progressively breathless.

However, a much more dramatic form of pulmonary embolus is where a large clot suddenly blocks a major artery within the pulmonary tree. If this cuts off the blood supply sufficiently the patient may die instantaneously. If the patient initially survives a large clot, it may be necessary to remove the clot urgently. This can be done rarely by surgery, or by infusing streptokinase directly into the pulmonary artery.

Even if the offending clot is removed, the treatment of pulmonary embolism is with long term anticoagulants starting with heparin and then warfarin. In the majority of cases with pulmonary embolism the treatment with heparin and warfarin only is an attempt to prevent further clots occurring and causing more damage. The original clots are gradually lysed (removed) by the body's own mechanisms and the patient's symptoms will get better.

The patient is usually breathless during the initial phase of pulmonary emboli, but over a period of time, often 3–4 weeks, the breathlessness gradually ceases. Because the clots block the blood supply to the lining of the lung – the pleura – pulmonary emboli may cause pain of a pleuritic nature. When this happens, the diagnosis lies between pulmonary emboli and pleurisy.

When the symptom is only progressive breathlessness, the diagnosis of pulmonary emboli can be easily forgotten. The patient's gradual recovery after pulmonary emboli is always accompanied by a surprising amount of tiredness. If pulmonary emboli are suspected clinically the diagnosis can be made with an isotope scan. Isotopes are both administered to the blood stream and inhaled. This allows the observer to see if there is a mismatch between the inhaled air and the blood vessels. The chest X-ray is of little value in this condition and the ECG less so.

After the first episode of pulmonary emboli, it is customary to anticoagulate for about six months, but after a second episode of emboli it may be appropriate to consider lifetime anticoagulation.

Once a patient has been diagnosed as having a pulmonary embolus, one must seek its source. Sometimes this is obvious, eg a deep vein thrombosis of the legs or after an abdominal operation, where the iliac veins have become damaged and an embolus forms just below the beginning of the inferior vena cava.

It used to be common to develop a pulmonary embolus a few days after an operation, but now one frequently treats high risk patients with subcutaneous heparin to avoid this happening. Very rarely pulmonary emboli may occur in association with disseminated cancer and where there is an abnormal clotting problem within the blood.

One should note that pulmonary emboli occur from within the veins and emboli cannot reach the arterial systems.

DISSECTING AORTIC ANEURYSM

This occurs when blood passes into the media of the aorta, destroys it and causes the inside and the outside layers to separate. In this way the dissection may extend from just above the aortic cusps, right round the aorta to the iliac arteries. Dissection of the ascending aorta causes severe chest pain which can mimic a myocardial infarction and, as it may often occur in patients with high blood pressure, there may well be confusion over the diagnosis. A dissecting aneurysm differs from a myocardial infarction when there is usually a normal ECG and the blood pressure tends to rise rather than fall. The dissection may involve the arteries which come off the aorta, eg the carotid arteries, spinal arteries, coronary arteries and renal arteries, by causing constriction at their origin.

The ideal investigation for dissection is the CT or MRI scan. Both will clearly demonstrate the dissection and its extent. Dissecting aneurysms have a high mortality depending on type, and although some can be treated conservatively (control BP and wait) most will require a major operation with possible bypass surgery if the patient is young and fit enough. Results are not good.

PERICARDITIS

Pericarditis is an inflammatory reaction in the tissue which surrounds the heart. The sac which contains the heart, the pericardium, is extremely sensitive and pericardial pain is very unpleasant indeed. The pain is central but usually relieved by leaning forward or being in one particular position. It is worse with breathing but can mimic that of a myocardial infarction.

Pericarditis will accompany myocardial infarctions in approximately 10–20% of cases although many of these will be transient and very mild. The commonest cause of pericarditis in the community is benign recurrent viral pericarditis which can usually be treated by non-steroidal, anti-inflammatory agents such as Voltarol or Brufen. There is an enormous number of causes of pericarditis from infections to neoplasms and collagen diseases, and the further treatment of this condition depends on the underlying cause.

PERICARDIAL EFFUSION AND TAMPONADE

Pericardial effusion is the presence of fluid within the pericardial sac, but outside the heart. In most people there is probably 20cc of serous fluid in this sac in normal circumstances, but in a number of conditions this can become considerably greater. In infectious diseases such as tuberculosis a pericardial effusion can be as much as several litres. This can occur because the pericardium has plenty of time to stretch and enlarge.

If, however, the pericardial effusion is rapid, eg when a knife pierces the left ventricle from a stab wound, the blood pouring into the pericardial sac will compress the heart. This is called tamponade. The immediate relief of tamponade is to insert a needle into the pericardial space to withdraw the fluid. In an emergency situation this must be done rapidly, but a pericardial tap to make the diagnosis of a particular pericardial effusion is something which must be done with great care. When inserting a needle into the pericardial sac it is potentially possible to pierce the ventricular wall and cause a disaster. A pericardial tap is usually done with great care and should probably be performed where there is cardiac surgery available if something should go wrong. There is in an infinite number of causes of pericardial effusion similar to those of pericarditis.

TUMOURS OF THE HEART

Tumours of the heart are rare. Occasionally an atrial myxoma may present where a large, relatively benign mass develops in the atrium to the size of approximately 1in diameter. This tends to block the mitral valve and cause a variety of strange murmurs, but is easily diagnosed by echocardiography and can be relatively easily treated surgically.

Rarely, tumours of the left ventricle can form which are much more dangerous because they involve the muscle of the heart wall. Secondary spread from other tumours, eg cancer of the bronchus, may occur towards the heart, but are usually in the pericardium. This may sometimes be associated with pericardial effusion.

AIDS

In AIDS, cardiac involvement occurs in up to a quarter of the patients, although many of these are only noted at post-mortem. Generally, about 10% of the patients with AIDS will present with some form of heart problems, the commonest of which is a dilated cardiomyopathy. Myocarditis may develop due to opportunistic infections, but the HIV virus itself causes a gradual reduction in function of the myocardium, giving congestive cardiac failure. Pericarditis, endocarditis and arrhythmias may also occur.

JOINT DISEASE AND THE HEART

A number of joint diseases can affect the heart in various ways. Most of these are also systemic and affect not only the joints but other parts of the body. Ankylosing spondylitis can result in damage to the aortic valve and aortic regurgitation. Rheumatoid arthritis can damage the mitral and aortic valves and polyarteritis nodosa, scleroderma and systemic lupus erythematosus can all damage the heart muscle and create a cardiomyopathy. When any inflammatory joint disease flares up, it is possible to get a myocarditis and possible pericarditis.

HEART DISEASE AND ENDOCRINE DISORDERS

An underactive thyroid will result in a slow pulse, low blood pressure and raised cholesterol which will cause early coronary artery disease. The ECG is normally low voltage and characteristic.

Hyperthyroidism causes the heart to race and the patient may develop atrial fibrillation. In Cushing's disease there is an excessive production of steroids, resulting in high blood pressure and congestive cardiac failure. Addison's disease is a lack of steroids within the body and causes a very low blood pressure with syncope due to postural hypotension.

A phaeochromocytoma, a tumour producing large quantities of catecholamines (eg adrenaline) may cause high blood pressure, sometimes episodic, and palpitations. There are other rarer endocrine disorders which affect the heart.

ARTERIOSCLEROSIS

It is important to distinguish arteriosclerosis from atherosclerosis. Atherosclerosis infers the narrowing of arteries due to laying down of cholesterol, etc., within the arteries, whereas arteriosclerosis is the hardening of arteries and the loss of their elasticity. Arteriosclerosis occurs in the elderly patients when the arteries change from being flexible tubes into rigid pipes, resulting in a wide pulse pressure and often a high systolic pressure. Arteriosclerosis and high blood pressure are associated with strokes, etc., but treatment of arteriosclerotic high blood pressure is quite difficult and sometimes impossible.

HEART DISEASE IN PREGNANCY

The commonest problem to affect cardiologists in this area is pre-eclamptic toxaemia (PET). This is a rise of blood pressure generally in the last third of pregnancy, which is part of a generalised condition that can result in both foetal and maternal deaths. Control of the blood pressure by various tablets, usually beta-blockers, is part of the treatment of the syndrome generally, but this is a specialised area usually controlled by obstetricians.

Idiopathic high blood pressure can present for the first time during pregnancy, and of course patients with established high blood pressure can become pregnant. All these aspects of high blood pressure must be carefully monitored, and if necessary the patient must be admitted to hospital for bed rest which helps to control the blood pressure.

It is common in pregnancy to have a heart murmur diagnosed. This is because the heart has to do about 30% more work to cope with the developing foetus, especially in the last third of pregnancy. Therefore, each stroke volume is greater and more blood comes streaming through the aortic valve. As it does so, a degree of turbulence may occur causing an innocent flow murmur. Murmurs in pregnancy should be diagnosed by echocardiography in view of the serious nature of problems which may occur if there is a valve lesion.

Patients with known valve lesions should receive antibiotic prophylaxis during delivery. Mild arrhythmias are also common in pregnancy, especially sinus tachycardias and ectopic beats. These are innocent and can be dealt with by reassurance.

Becoming pregnant with major heart disease is something which must be dealt with extremely carefully and is entirely dependent upon the individual and the heart disease in question.

TRAVELLING ABROAD

Holidays are generally more beneficial than risky for cardiac patients unless the disease is severe. The two main problems are flying and being abroad.

Flying

Most airlines will provide wheelchairs, etc, for patients who need them if informed in advance with an accompanying doctor's letter. In some cases the airline will require a further doctor's letter giving the patient permission to travel.

Anxiety is a major problem for passengers as it can precipitate problems such as angina. Tranquillisers or beta-blockers taken shortly before take off may be valuable.

Patients often worry about the oxygen pressure in the cabin, which may fall from approximately 100mmHg at sea level to 75mmHg at high altitude. For the patient without serious heart failure or co-existing lung disease this is not a problem. At 75mmHg the blood is still 98% saturated with oxygen. If dyspnoea develops due to apparent lack of air, oxygen masks can be available for those with heart failure. Those with lung disease and carbon dioxide retention are special cases requiring specific medical advice.

Because cabin air is usually dry, patients may become dehydrated, especially if they are on diuretics for heart failure. These patients should be advised to drink adequate fluid but not alcohol.

Inactivity on the plane may result in a deep venous thrombosis (DVT) of the leg. To avoid this, patients at risk should drink adequate non-alcoholic fluids, walk around the plane every half an hour and flex their calf muscles periodically. When sitting down, long sleeps should be avoided as the legs may become completely immobile. Patients most at risk are those who have had a previous DVT.

Being abroad

The fear of falling ill in a foreign country is common, especially after a recent cardiac illness. Patients should have adequate medical insurance, enough medication to last at least a week longer than the holiday (to take account of flight delays) and a letter from the doctor giving a brief outline of their diagnosis and treatment. It is advisable to find out the altitude of the holiday destination or any excursions from it. Most heart patients should not go higher than 8,000 feet. Heat, gastrointestinal upsets and antibiotics may all upset warfarin levels in anticoagulated patients. If a patient is away for more than about three weeks, he should probably have a blood test to check his anticoagulation.

NON-CARDIAC SURGERY IN THE CARDIAC PATIENT

Introduction

A doctor is often asked what risks patients take when they require a hernia operation for example and are known to have cardiac problems. Statistics for this type of situation are not readily available, and of course each case must be assessed on its own merits. If an operation is essential, eg for cancer, a different view will prevail compared to an elective operation, eg varicose veins. There are some general points about the operation which are important.

(a) The patient must receive a good anaesthetic from a good anaesthetist and be carefully monitored. Above all the patient should not have a sudden increase in pre-load or after-load on his heart and both tachycardias and bradycardias must be avoided. A well organised anaesthetist will avoid these problems or enable them to be dealt with as quickly as possible.

(b) Pre-operative cardiac tests, eg ECG, exercise test and echocardiography, should be performed if there is uncertainty about the degree of cardiac abnormality.

(c) Treatment for existing heart conditions should not be stopped during the peri-operative period. If oral treatment is not possible, eg after bowel surgery, drugs should be given intravenously or percutaneously.

(d) The choice of anaesthetic agent is important. Halothane is more likely to depress LV function and lower the blood pressure than other anaesthetic gases. Nitric oxide is the least likely to cause problems.

Risks of particular cardiac problems

Angina

For convenience, angina can be graded from I to IV according to the New York Heart Association classification. Class I and II are mild to moderate and classes III and IV are moderate to severe and unstable angina respectively. Class I and II angina rarely increase the risk of an operation, but from moderately severe angina to unstable angina the increased risk will range from 3–20%. Patients should therefore be carefully examined pre-operatively and beta-blockers added, where appropriate, to cope with the stress of the operation.

Myocardial infarction

Taken overall, the current operation risk at three months in an uncomplicated myocardial infarction is about 6% and at six months approximately 2.5%.

Valvular disease

The risk in these cases depends mainly on the state of the left ventricle. Poor left ventricular function associated with valve disease may increase the risk markedly; eg with moderately severe aortic stenosis the risk with good heart muscle is about 3% but with poor function approximately 15%.

High blood pressure

An enormous number of operations are cancelled every year because of high blood pressure, much of which is due to anxiety. Only when the diastolic blood pressure is at a fairly constant 110mmHg will significant blood pressure changes occur.

Heart failure

Most cases of heart failure (70%) occur within one hour of the operation due to too much fluid or blood being given to a patient during the operation.

Prosthetic heart valves

Great care must be taken if a patient has a prosthetic valve replacement and is on warfarin. Stopping the warfarin will allow the wound to heal but also allow the valve to clot. Careful use of intravenous heparin which can be 'switched on and off' is normally the preferred method of controlling this situation.

Antibiotics

In a patient with valvular heart disease great care is made to avoid infection with prophylactic antibiotics.

THE HEART AND ILLICIT DRUGS

Introduction

Drugs such as cocaine, amphetamines, ecstasy, lysergic acid diamide (LSD) and pencyclidine hydrochloride (PCP) exert their predominant effect by raising the level of adrenaline within the blood stream. This gives a feeling of excitement and lifting of the spirits, but at the same time will cause a tachycardia and rise in the blood pressure. This is usually well tolerated in young people with normal hearts, but clearly could be dangerous with anyone with potential heart problems. Opiates such as morphine and pethidine work in different ways, but can still produce abnormal heart rhythms, while solvent abuse is predominantly similar to alcohol intoxication with at least half the deaths being caused by arrhythmias.

Individual drugs

Cocaine

Cocaine blocks the uptake of adrenaline, increasing its concentration enough to cause coronary vasospasm. This in turn may result in a myocardial infarction. In addition, cocaine can have a direct effect upon the myocardium, causing the development of a dilated cardiomyopathy. In those who die of cocaine use, nearly a quarter show evidence of inflammation of heart muscle. Any patient who has taken cocaine and developed severe chest pain should be referred to hospital immediately. In a series of 70 such patients, half either had a myocardial infarction or definite transient angina. The route of cocaine absorption is not relevant in the incidence of heart disease, so that snorting cocaine can be as dangerous as intravenous cocaine.

Ecstasy

Like cocaine, this results in a tachycardia and cardiac arrhythmias. Its use at parties adds dehydration to this effect, resulting in hyperthermia and sudden death. Sudden hypertensive crises are also reported.

Amphetamines

Amphetamines particularly promote high levels of catecholamines, causing an increase of blood pressure and heart rate with subsequent arrhythmias and cardiac failure.

Lysergic acid diamide

LSD produces a marked rise in adrenaline over quite a long period of time, giving high blood pressure and tachycardia.

Pencyclidine hydrochloride

Usual doses of PCP cause a rise in blood pressure and heart rate; large amounts can result in convulsions and coma.

Opiates

These are less likely to cause heart problems, although cardiac arrhythmias have been reported with a prolonged QT syndrome.

Cannabis

Cannabis raises the catecholamines as well, causing a tachycardia and raised blood pressure. Prolonged use has the same effect as smoking cigarettes on the heart but to a greater degree.

Solvent abuse

This can cause a sudden slowing of the heart, respiratory depression and cardiac arrhythmias.

General

Any drug user who injects himself runs the risk of introducing infection, particularly *Staphylococci*, into the blood stream which can result in endocarditis on the tricuspid or pulmonary valves. The mortality of this is about 10%, but it will have long term effects upon the quality of life of the patient who survives.

INDEX

Page numbers in *italics* or **bold** indicate a figure or table respectively, appearing away from its page